Faith Journey through Fantasy Lands

Faith Journey through

Fantasy Lands

A Christian Dialogue with Harry Potter, Star Wars, and The Lord of the Rings

Russell W. Dalton

FAITH JOURNEY THROUGH FANTASY LANDS
A Christian Dialogue with Harry Potter, *Star Wars,* and *The Lord of the Rings*

Large-quantity purchases or custom editions of this book are available at a discount from the publisher. For more information, contact the sales department at Augsburg Fortress, Publishers, 1-800-328-4648, or write to: Sales Director, Augsburg Fortress, Publishers, P.O. Box 1209, Minneapolis, MN 55440-1209.

ISBN 0-8066-4571-7

Cover design by Brad Norr
Book design by Michelle L. N. Cook

The paper used in this publication meets the minimum requirements of American National Standard for Information Sciences—Permanence of Paper for Printed Library Materials, ANSI Z329.48-1984. ♾ ™

Manufactured in the U.S.A.

07 06 05 04 03 1 2 3 4 5 6 7 8 9 10

This book is dedicated to my big brother, Bob,
who introduced me to Middle-earth,
showed me the Star Wars universe,
shared his enthusiasm for Hogwarts,
and best of all, taught me about the Reign of God.
It is also dedicated to my children,
Nathan, Anna Grace, and Maria,
who were very patient and supportive
while their dad was at home yet still at work on this book.
Though they have just begun their journeys,
they are already heroes.

Contents

Our cinema screens, video stores, and bookstores are bombarded with tales of wizards, magic, and battles between good and evil. The Harry Potter stories, the *Star Wars* films, and *The Lord of the Rings* trilogy create vivid worlds of fantasy. Many Christians have enjoyed these books and have even discovered in them spiritual themes that have enriched their devotional lives. Many others have serious concerns about some aspects of one or all of these series and have avoided them. How should Christians respond? This book advocates an approach that neither condemns these stories nor accepts them as gospel. Instead, it places these stories in a dialogue with the Christian faith, so that we can explore them and at the same time stay connected to our own faith traditions.

This book explores today's fantasy stories as a way for Christians to reflect on their own faith journeys. It uses the image of a journey, or quest, as it is depicted in these stories to help explore several aspects of the Christian life. Each chapter looks at spiritual motifs found in the fantasy stories as a way to identify our spiritual yearnings or raise religious issues that are relevant to our own faith journeys. Each chapter then compares the way these issues are explored in the fantasy stories with the way they are explored in the Bible. The Gospels and their description of the faith journeys of Jesus and his disciples are given special attention. Along the way this book also provides Christians with connections and common ground that will help them share their own faith journeys with their children or friends who may be more interested in talking about Harry Potter, *Star Wars,* and *The Lord of the Rings* than about the Bible or their own Christian journey.

Faith Journey through Fantasy Lands also examines some of the concerns that these stories have raised for their fans and for apprehensive parents and teachers. Those who are most interested in these issues may wish to start by reading the special section at the end of the book, "Dangers along the Path." This section steps outside the stories and takes a closer look at some controversies surrounding them, such as the use of sorcery, the questionable conduct of some characters, the obsessive behavior of some fans, and more. Some readers may be reassured by what they read, finding that they need not be overly concerned regarding some aspects of these stories. Others may find that this section raises some cautions and concerns that they had not previously considered. In either case, readers will have the opportunity to reflect on their own concerns and to better understand the reservations of others.

This book is designed to be used either for individual reflection or by groups, such as college or seminary classes, Sunday school classes, and other study groups. Each chapter closes with questions for reflection, which can be used by individuals or as group discussion questions. The book can serve as the basis of a weekly study series, by reading and discussing one or more chapters each week. For those who have not seen the films or as a review for those who may have read the books or watched the films some time ago, groups may wish to gather to watch the first film in each series before starting their study.

Faith Journey through Fantasy Lands assumes that the reader has at least a general familiarity with Harry Potter, *Star Wars,* and *The Lord of the Rings,* so it will be most accessible to those who have read at least the first book or watched the first film of each series. But readers do not need to have an exhaustive knowledge of these stories to benefit from this book. Although I have tried not to reveal too many details of the concluding scenes of the stories, readers should be forewarned that this book contains some spoilers that reveal major plot points. If you are in the middle of reading one of the novels or about to watch one of the films discussed here, you may wish to finish them before you read this book.

At the time of this writing, the series that serve as the focus of this book include five Harry Potter novels, five *Star Wars* films, *The Hobbit,* and *The Lord of the Rings* trilogy. Clearly not everything in these fourteen stories that is consistent with or contrary to the Christian life can be covered in one book, but it is my hope that the thoughts shared here will inspire readers to make more connections of their own.

Not all Christians will share the same opinion of today's fantasy stories or the views offered in this book. Some Christians have embraced these stories, while others oppose them as a matter of faith. One of my goals in writing this book has been to invite readers into a thoughtful dialogue with these stories. I hope that this dialogue will help readers arrive at their own opinions and at the same time help them understand other viewpoints and respect other people's right to disagree.

In *The Lord of the Rings,* Frodo, Sam, Pippin, and Merry enter a world of elves, dwarves, trolls, and orcs. At the end of their journey, they return from that experience to their home in the "real world," ennobled to be heroes. Perhaps we too can journey into these fictional fantasy lands and find our way back from our travels ennobled to live out our faith in new ways. My hope is that you will enjoy the experience and be enriched by it. Welcome to the journey!

Acknowledgments

Writing this book has been a journey in and of itself, and I have had many traveling companions who have helped me on the way. I would like to thank my colleagues at United Theological Seminary in Dayton, Ohio, for their support and encouragement as I wrote this book. I also wish to thank my research assistant, Tracy Zielinski, who drew on her extensive knowledge of these fantasy worlds to help improve the accuracy and suitability of the examples I used in the book. I am grateful to the supporters and staff of the Beavercreek branch of the Greene County Public Library, who cheerfully kept me supplied with books, videos, and audiotapes as I did my research. I wish to thank Marilyn Kielbasa, the development editor for the book, who helped polish my sentences and caught several errors. I am also indebted to Michael Wilt, acquisitions editor at Augsburg Books, who supported this project from its inception and gave me valuable suggestions and guidance as we worked together to see it to its completion. Thanks to Michelle L. N. Cook, assistant managing editor for Augsburg Books, for graciously allowing me to add some reflections on the latest Harry Potter novel at the eleventh hour after this book was already in its proof form. Finally, I wish to thank my wise, fearless, and fair wife, Lisa. She proofread every chapter and, because she knows my mind better than anyone, offered advice that helped me express my thoughts more clearly. Her support and encouragement have been nothing less than heroic.

Christian Approaches to Fantasy and Fiction

Why Should Christians Care about Fantasy Stories?

Why should Christians care about fantasy stories? The word *fantasy,* after all, is commonly understood to mean "frivolous" or "false." But the word is also used to refer to a genre of creative and imaginative stories that explore serious spiritual issues. Like the legends or myths of old, fantasy stories can help us step outside our world to see it in new ways.

Christian storytellers have a long tradition of using fantasy stories to explore Christian themes in new settings. Fantasy's motifs of heroism, virtue, and supernatural events make it well suited for this task. The legends of King Arthur and the wizard Merlin explore the notions of heroism and sacrifice with reference to Christian beliefs and virtues. In the seventeenth and eighteenth centuries, John Bunyan's *Pilgrim's Progress* was the only book, other than the Bible, that many English-speaking Christians owned. It told the story of a Christian life as though it was a fantastic journey from the City of Destruction to the Heavenly Palaces. In the late nineteenth century, Christian novelist George MacDonald wrote fantasy tales, including *Lilith, Phatastes,* and *The Golden Key,* which creatively explored aspects of Christian theology and the Christian life. MacDonald's novels inspired C. S. Lewis, whose fantasy novels, such as the seven books of the Chronicles of Narnia series and *Till We Have Faces,* have encouraged Christians in their spiritual lives for decades. Even today, shelves of Christian bookstores are filled with new fictional and fantastical accounts of past and future worlds.

But what about those fantasy stories that are not explicitly Christian in their content? Why should Christians care about them? First of all, our concern for people around us should move us to care about fantasy stories. The stories this book focuses on—the Harry Potter stories, the *Star Wars* films, *The Hobbit,* and *The Lord of the Rings*—have become some of the most popular books and films of our time. Because today's fantasy stories (for the sake of brevity, I will often refer to these three series simply as "today's fantasy stories") are so popular, they tell us not only about their authors but also about the culture that has embraced them. We could say that these books and films serve as "artifacts" of today's culture, and give us insight into the thoughts, yearnings, and beliefs of our times. Any time a movie, song, book, or television show becomes this popular, we should take notice so we can better understand our culture and our neighbors who live in it.

For many readers and viewers, these fantasy stories provide more than light entertainment. The stories resonate with them because they speak to deeply spiritual aspects of their lives, such as the meaning of life and death, morality, and even the fate of creation. Because of these connections, these stories have elicited great devotion and interest among their fans. In October 2001, the BBC reported that enough people in the United Kingdom wrote in "Jedi Knight" as their religion on their census forms that the government plans to include it on the list of religions for the next census. Although we may suspect that many of people who wrote in this religion did so at least partly in jest, they still took no other religion seriously enough to list it on their form. Many people with little or no connection to organized religion have said that they use one or more of today's fantasy series as religious texts of sorts. They watch them or read them partly to help them reflect on the spiritual aspects of their own lives. For these reasons

Christians who care about the spiritual life of others should explore these stories and not ignore them.

Second, we should care about these stories not only because they can help us understand others but for our own benefit as well. Throughout the centuries Christians have engaged the popular culture that surrounded them, and reflected on the connections that could be made between their culture and their faith. Many Bible scholars believe that Jesus, for example, told stories that his hearers already would have known and then put his own spiritual twist on them. For instance, the story that Jesus told of the man who found a treasure in a field, hid it, and then sold all that he had to buy that field may well have been circulating around Galilee at the time. It is a fascinating story, even if the man's actions do seem a bit underhanded, and Jesus did not shy away from using it. Instead, he used it first to engage his audience and then to make a point about the Reign of God (Matt. 13:44).

The Apostle Paul actively engaged the culture in which he lived as well. When Paul addressed the Areopagus in Athens (Acts 17:16–34), he earned the right to speak to them by establishing his knowledge of their cultural texts. He quotes the philosopher Epimenides ("In him we live and move and have our being") and the poet Aratus ("For we too are his offspring"). He had obviously studied these non-Christian and non-Jewish writers and reflected on how their writings related to his own faith. In addition, he saw how he could use their writings to establish a common ground with his audience. Although Paul clearly did not agree with everything these authors wrote, he found insights in their writings that helped him reflect on his own faith and better communicate that faith to the people around him.[1]

We can all benefit from engaging the stories of our culture. By reading, watching, and reflecting on the Harry Potter series, the *Star Wars* films, and *The Lord of the Rings,* we can better understand the world around us and perhaps come to better understand and articulate our own faith as well.

Yes, But Are These Stories "Christian"?

Are these stories Christian? Actually, that may not be the most useful question to ask. Some Christians, however, approach a film or a novel with the goal of determining whether it is "Christian" or not, and consequently whether it is suitable to be read or watched by Christians. Different people use different criteria to determine this, and it may be helpful to examine today's fantasy stories using these criteria before moving toward a different approach.

The most limiting criterion some people use is to determine if a book or film is specifically and exclusively "Christian." Those who take this approach tend to trust only books and films that are produced by Christians and intended for Christian education or evangelistic purposes, such as products found in Christian bookstores. If we use this criterion then none of the fantasy series that are the focus of this book would be considered fit for use by Christians. J. K. Rowling is a member of the Church of Scotland.[2] She has done good works, such as supporting a number of charities, and in her younger days, worked for two years for Amnesty International researching human rights issues in Africa.[3] Still, while many have noticed Christian themes and biblical allusions in her books, there are no explicitly Christian messages or evangelistic purpose in her stories.

Because George Lucas, the creator of *Star Wars,* draws on many faith traditions and a variety of myths to shape his stories, adherents of nearly every major religion, including Christianity, have claimed that the *Star Wars* saga illustrates the tenets of their religion. Still, the *Star Wars* series is not a specifically Christian series. As a matter of fact, many scholars see more parallels in the films with Taoism than with Christianity. Lucas has said that his *Star Wars* films are not intended to promote or establish any specific religion, but instead are designed to get young people to think about spiritual things in general.[4] Lucas believes that value exists in established organized religions. He fears the prospect that popular entertainment such as his films might take the place of organized religion because he believes that they provide too thin a base for theology.[5]

Of the three creators of these fantasy series, one is most tempted to see J. R. R. Tolkien as a "Christian" author. J. R. R. Tolkien was a Roman Catholic who helped lead C. S. Lewis to a Christian faith. But unlike Lewis and the Chronicles of Narnia, Tolkien did not write *The Lord of the Rings* as an allegory of the Christian faith with a specifically Christian message. As a matter of fact, Tolkien stated that although he did not want his story to be inconsistent with Christian beliefs, he did not feel under any obligation to make the story fit into any particular Christian theology.[6]

Although these stories are not specifically Christian by this first criterion, they do explore a number of spiritual themes that are important to Christians. For some Christians it can be disconcerting to find spiritual themes in books or films that are not explicitly Christian. Even relatively benign shows such as *Touched by an Angel* are sometimes criticized for not always naming Christ as the focus of their explorations of spiritual issues. In the past decade, many popular songs, TV programs, and movies have explored spiritual themes. And though they may not be specifically Christian, they do provide us with an opportunity to reflect on our own faith—as well as the spiritual issues that are on the minds of people today.

A second criterion some Christians use to evaluate works of fiction is the manner in which they portray Christians, churches, and other religious organizations.[7] In past decades many Christians have been troubled to see clergy and churchgoers portrayed in many films and television shows as hypocrites, judgmental busybodies, or naïve buffoons. The three fantasy series that this book focuses on have very few explicit references to Christianity or Christian practices. The *Star Wars* films and *The Lord of the Rings* trilogy take place in other worlds that apparently do not have an established Christian religion. Harry Potter's world is more like our own. The students at Hogwarts School of Witchcraft and Wizardry celebrate Christmas and have an Easter holiday, but there are no descriptions of characters actively involved in Christian worship or prayer. *Harry Potter and the Chamber of Secrets* does mention that Harry and Ron see churches in town as they fly Mr. Weasley's Ford Anglia overhead,[8] and in *Harry Potter and the Goblet of Fire,* an empty suit of armor is enchanted to sing "O Come All Ye Faithful" at Christmastime.[9] Still, little in the books can be taken as a positive or negative critique of Christianity or the Christian Church.[10]

By the criterion of how they depict Christians and the Christian Church, then, the Harry Potter stories, the *Star Wars* films, and *The Lord of the Rings* offer little to critique. They do not explicitly commend Christians or the Christian faith, nor do they have a consciously anti-Christian agenda.

Perhaps the most popular criterion Christians use to evaluate works of fiction centers on the morals and values evident in books and films.[11] Do they contain sex, violence, or profanity that is inappropriate for some or all viewers? Do the main characters act in ways that are consistent or inconsistent with Christian values?

How do Harry Potter, *Star Wars,* and *The Lord of the Rings* measure up by this standard? These films contain a fair amount of violence, but they have far less sexual content or profanity than most novels and films today. Many Christians see the behavior of the heroes in these stories to be quite consistent with Christian values. In the original *Star Wars* trilogy (that is, episodes 4, 5, and 6), the characters demonstrate loyalty and courageously stand up, in the face of great personal peril, for what is just. The characters in *The Lord of the Rings* are often lifted up as models of virtue. The Harry Potter series has elicited conflicting opinions. The editors of the periodical *Christianity Today* published an editorial titled, "Why we like Harry Potter: The series is a 'Book of Virtues' with a preadolescent funny bone."[12] Meanwhile, others have pointed out that the children in the Harry Potter stories frequently break school rules, lie to get out of trouble, and show disrespect to their elders.[13] These questionable virtues will be discussed in the final section of this book, "Dangers along the Path."

Should Christians, and Christian children in particular, be discouraged from reading books that are not explicitly Christian in their content? Many books and films today have extremely violent content or show explicit immoral behavior and offer little or no redeeming value. It makes sense to avoid these. But it is difficult in this media-saturated world to avoid everything that is not completely consistent with Christian beliefs. Perhaps a better approach is to practice discernment as we watch and read, and to teach discernment to our children. As a youth minister, some of my best youth group meetings were those in which I had teenagers bring in music videos taped from cable music stations. We watched and listened together "with our brains turned on." We would think about what we saw and heard, and discuss what we agreed with and what positive messages we could find, even in secular videos. Then we would discuss which of the images and ideas presented were inconsistent with our Christian beliefs. The teenagers were often surprised at what they saw, both positive and negative, in these videos. I was often surprised at how critical these teenagers would become of their own music and the video portrayals of that music. During these sessions we were teaching each other discernment and media literacy.

We must use discernment with whatever books we read or films we watch, and even as we read the Bible itself. The Bible is filled with sex and violence and includes many stories of immoral behavior by Bible heroes such as Jacob, Moses, King David, and others. These are not "go thou and do likewise" stories, but must be read and reflected on with discernment.

This book takes an approach that goes beyond a "thumbs up" or "thumbs down"[14] evaluation of fiction and film. It gives the reader a chance to reflect on whether or not the behaviors and beliefs of the characters in today's fantasy stories are consistent with the Christian faith, but it also looks at the questions these stories demand of our faith by entering into a dialogue between these fantasy stories and the Christian story.

Dialoguing with Fiction and Film

The goal of a dialogue is not simply to find out whether we agree or disagree with the material and stop there. If we are talking with people and find that we do not agree with them on every point, we usually do not respond by simply turning our backs and walking away from them. Dialogues can be much more rewarding than that. As a matter of fact, the best dialogue partners are often those who may share some of the same interests and concerns that we do, but approach them from a slightly different perspective. If we only talked with those who agreed with us on everything, then conversations would be dull; we would never be challenged or learn anything new.

Films and novels do not just present the world as it is. They present the world in a way that reflects certain assumptions and values, which may or may not be consistent with our own Christian beliefs and values. When we engage works of fiction critically, we are exercising our Christian faith. Bryan P. Stone, author of *Faith and Film,* has called this "an interfaith dialogue."[15] The goal of this dialogue is not simply to determine the message of a film or novel and then accept it as though it were gospel to us. Nor is the goal to read a novel or watch a film simply to hunt for illustrations of our own theological beliefs. Dialogues are more complex than that. Dialogues, whether with people or with works of fiction, involve conversation and give and take. They can provide us with new perspectives on aspects of our faith that have become overly familiar and open our eyes to aspects of our faith that we may not have seen otherwise.[16]

Today's fantasy stories share many of our spiritual concerns, but they also offer us a fresh perspective. They can remind us of aspects of our Christian story that we may have overlooked, and allow us to appreciate familiar aspects of our faith in new ways.

Ancient Myths and Contemporary Fantasy Stories As Spiritual Journeys

The Harry Potter stories, *Star Wars,* and *The Lord of the Rings* serve as modern-day myths that explore some of the same spiritual motifs as the legends and myths of old. They tell tales of spiritual quests that have been told since the days of yore. All three of the authors of these fantasy stories drew on mythology to construct their tales, and they follow many of the same common mythic patterns.

J. K. Rowling follows mythic patterns in her Harry Potter stories. In addition, she uses names from Greek and Roman myths, such as Hermione and Minerva, and populates her world with a wide variety of mythical creatures, such as dragons, trolls, three-headed guard dogs, centaurs, basilisks, griffins, and more. George Lucas drew on Joseph Campbell's well-known work in mythology[17] to outline his *Star Wars* tales. Lucas has said: "I'm telling an old myth in a new way. That's how you pass on the meat and potatoes of your society to the next generation."[18] J. R. R. Tolkien drew on his studies of fourth- and fifth-century Anglo-Saxon history and legend to construct Middle-earth. His goal was to create a new mythology for England, a sweeping epic that would echo the themes of ancient myths.

Throughout the ages, humankind has constructed myths and legends as a way to explore the ultimate spiritual questions of life. Although these myths come from many different places and cultures, they share similar motifs. In many myths the heroes are called to adventure by a mysterious stranger, receive special gifts for their quest, meet a group of companions and friends, make their way through a dark forest, descend into the depths to face the evil one, make a great sacrifice, and emerge victorious.

Many people believe that the reason these myths share so many common themes and motifs is that they express deeply understood truths about the human experience and our visions of that which is divine. These mythic motifs are seen as archetypical, or "bred in the bone," of humankind. From a Christian perspective, we might say that God created these spiritual motifs in us. We all share a yearning to find purpose and meaning in our lives and to know our God. Taking this perspective, it is not surprising to find stories of miracles, sons of gods, virgin births, sacrifices, deaths, and resurrections in ancient myths from around the world, as well as in the Bible.

Christians find the ultimate fulfillment of the spiritual yearnings expressed in these myths in the Gospel story of Jesus Christ.

Incidentally, it was an insight similar to this that changed the life of the famous fantasy writer C. S. Lewis. Lewis was very moved by the profound spiritual truths he found in the ancient myths of dying and reviving gods, such as Balder the brave, Adonis, and Bacchus; yet he was very resistant to the Gospel story of Jesus Christ's death and resurrection. Lewis could not accept the Gospel story, because he knew that its message was paralleled by many ancient myths. How could such a mythic story be true? Lewis's skepticism troubled his friends J. R. R. Tolkien and Henry Victor Dyson. One fateful September evening in 1931, Tolkien and Dyson stayed up talking with Lewis late into the evening and into the next morning. Tolkien argued that the myths Lewis found so moving ultimately came from God and were God's way of expressing great truths. As a matter of fact, he argued, all great stories pointed toward the greatest story of all, the Gospel story of Jesus Christ. Tolkien believed that at the core of Christianity was a myth that was also a fact. As he would later write in his famous essay "On Fairy Stories": "[T]his story is supreme; and it is true. God is the Lord of angels, and of men—and of elves. Legend and History have met and fused."[19]

This line of reasoning had a great impact on Lewis, and helped him come to a place where he could embrace the Christian faith as his own. As Lewis would write in a letter to Arthur Greeves, he came to believe that "the story of Christ is simply a true myth."[20] The "pagan stories," he wrote, were God's way of expressing Godself through the minds of the poets, while the Christ story was God's way of expressing Godself through "real things."[21]

Today many Christians find it helpful to look back at the ancient myths in order to explore deep truths in new ways. They look at the ways myths treat religious themes, and compare them to the ways our Christian traditions treat them. We can do the same thing as we examine today's fantasy stories. Each chapter of this book explores a motif that is found in ancient myths and in today's fantasy stories, such as the call of the hero,[22] the provisions given to the hero for the journey, the trail of trials, and more. Each chapter then turns to the way this motif is addressed by the Christian biblical tradition, with special attention paid to the journey of Jesus' disciples as it is depicted in the Gospels.[23]

The Harry Potter stories, the *Star Wars* films, and *The Lord of the Rings* all tell tales of fascinating journeys and heroic quests. But these are nothing compared to the very real adventure of faith that God calls us to undertake. This book is designed to offer readers an opportunity to look at their life as a heroic journey of faith. These journeys are dangerous, and we must have courage to complete them. But if we accept our calling and follow God's path, we will be embarking on the most amazing adventure of all.

Questions for Reflection

Think of a book or film that was not explicitly Christian but has inspired you. What about that book or film spoke to you the most?

Recall a conversation that you had with someone who disagreed with you. How did it challenge you? How did it help you to rethink your own position or to reaffirm your position on the topic?

Recall an ancient myth or legend that you may have read or heard. Can you think of any parallels between that story and the story of Jesus and his disciples?

What have you heard from Christian friends regarding Harry Potter, *Star Wars,* and *The Lord of the Rings?* Has it all been positive? Has it all been negative? Has it been a mixture of the two? What were some of the positive comments? What were some of the negative comments?

A Whole New World

When I was in college, I served as a student leader in the campus ministry. One day a young man whom I had never met came to me. "I was told you could help me," he said. "And you'd better, or I'm checking out." His eyes were red from crying, but his voice was filled with anger and defiance. He agreed to meet with me, and we talked in my attic apartment. He said that we lived in a dark and meaningless world, and that he believed that if there was a God then God was only there to judge him for who he was and what he had done. I did not deny him his sorrow or his anger, but told him that according to the Christian faith, God is known as a God of grace and forgiveness. At first he could not accept that this was true. It was not the message he had heard from any of the Christians that he knew. But as I opened up the Scriptures and we read passage after passage, he came to recognize that God was indeed a God of grace who forgave him and accepted him for who he was. In that attic he prayed and accepted God's grace in his life. I will always remember his reaction as we left my apartment and walked out onto the sunny campus. "It's like I'm walking into a whole new world, Russ," he said. "It's a whole new world."

One of the joys of reading or watching fantasy tales such as the Harry Potter stories, *Star Wars,* or *The Lord of the Rings* is that we feel as though we are being transported into a whole new world. Harry Potter lives in a world of muggles and Quidditch matches. He travels to places such as Diagon Alley, Gringotts bank, and Hogwarts, and meets goblins, trolls, dragons, griffins, and centaurs along the way. In the *Star Wars* films, Luke Skywalker travels across a galaxy, from the desert planet of Tatooine to places such as the snow-covered world of Hoth, the swamps of Dagobah, the Forest Moon of Endor, and beyond. He encounters Jawas, Wookies, a wampa ice creature, Ewoks, and more. In *The Lord of the Rings,* Frodo Baggins braves dark riders, orcs, a Balrog, and a giant spider. His journey takes him from Hobbiton of the Shire, through the Mines of Moria under the Misty Mountains, into the trees of Lothlórien, and to the Cracks of Doom in Mordor itself.

One of the most attractive qualities of these stories is that they are set in fully realized fantasy worlds. J. K. Rowling knows much more about the world that she has created than the parts that have found their way into her books. She even released two of the fictional textbooks that appear in her stories, *Quidditch through the Ages,*[1] and *Fantastic Beasts and Where to Find Them.*[2] These books gave fans of the series more insight into Harry's world and at the same time raised money for charity.

Many *Star Wars* fans know the minutest details about the characters, histories, planets, and technology of the *Star Wars* universe. Their knowledge of these worlds goes far beyond what can be gleaned from watching the films alone. The series has spawned a number of novels, detailed encyclopedias, and guides to the characters, planets, and creatures.

But it is J. R. R. Tolkien who is often credited with inventing the modern fantasy novel, through his creation of Middle-earth. Tolkien painted Middle-earth with such deep colors, including an ancient epic history, vivid geography, and elaborate languages and cultures, that many readers came away with the impression that it somehow really existed in a way that other fictional worlds did not. George R. R. Martin observed that it was not a poster of Tolkien's characters that fans of *The Lord of the Rings* taped to their dorm room walls; it was a map.[3] It was not just the characters or plot that captured the reader's attention; it was the world itself.

What is the nature of these worlds? What makes them so fascinating that readers and viewers keep going back to them again and again? How do these worlds compare to the world as it is described in the Gospels? This chapter looks at the nature of these fantasy lands and compares them to the world of our own faith journeys.

Seeing Our World in a Whole New Way

The main characters in these fantasy stories find themselves entering into a wider world, and they each do so in a different way. As *Harry Potter and the Sorcerer's Stone* begins, Harry does not know that there is a whole other world of wizards and magic within his world.[4] He is surprised to hear that it exists, but he accepts and embraces it so quickly that we suspect that on some level he must have known that it existed all along. Harry begins to remember causing strange things to happen and meeting odd people on the street. As he learns more about the wizarding world, his own world begins to make more sense.

In *Star Wars: A New Hope* (1977),[5] Luke Skywalker knew there was more to the universe than his simple life on Tatooine. He longed to go out into the galaxy and experience life there. Still, he was not aware of all that the universe had to offer. He is fascinated when old Ben Kenobi begins to tell him about the Force. Ben has Luke blind himself by putting down the blast shield of his helmet, and then has Luke try to deflect ray beams with his lightsaber. At first Luke is skeptical and misses the first few blasts. Then Luke begins to sense the Force and is able to deflect the next ray blasts despite his inability to see them. Ben tells him, "You've taken your first step into a larger world."

In *The Lord of the Rings,* Frodo and Sam had heard Bilbo's stories of life beyond the Shire, but dwarves, elves, and goblins were still characters in someone else's stories and songs. We get the impression that Frodo and Sam were fairly content to accept these aspects of their world in theory, but they did not expect to find themselves taking an active part in them.

Many Christians have had faith experiences that parallel those of Harry, Luke, or Frodo and Sam. Some come into the life of faith and it is a total surprise to them. They had failed to recognize the spiritual dimension of their lives, but in hindsight they can see that it was there all along. Others have an inkling that there is more to their world, but they can point to a moment in their lives when they entered into the life of faith on a deeper level. Still others were quite comfortable where they were. They were aware of the life of faith on some level, but can point to a time when they were called to move outside of their comfort zone and embrace life in a different way.

The Gospels tell us that Jesus came preaching a message that called his followers to understand their world in a whole new way as well. He called on them to recognize the Reign of God, a phrase more often translated "the Kingdom of God." The phrase "the Kingdom of God" can be misleading to today's readers, however, because Jesus was not preaching about just a future in heaven or a castle in the clouds. He was teaching and demonstrating the way life would be if God ruled; he was explaining the way things would be if things were done God's way. That is why he taught his followers to pray, "Thy Kingdom come, thy will be done, on earth as it is in heaven." As he began healing the sick and preaching the good news, he told his listeners that this Reign of God had come near (Mark 1:15). And Jesus told the Pharisees that they should not look to some future time when the Reign of God would come, "[f]or, in fact, the kingdom of God is among you" (Luke 17:21). Jesus called his followers to grab on to the Realm of God with the same passion as a person who would give up everything he owned in order to obtain a treasure or pearl of great price (Matt. 13:44–45).

Entering this new world takes courage. As exciting as it is, it takes us outside of our comfort zone. In the Book of Genesis, Abraham was called to leave the comfort of a world of provincial gods and journey forth into the unknown with God. In the same way, Jesus called his disciples to leave their religious comfort zones and take part in a movement of God's that had cosmic implications. He invited them to change the way they understood and engaged the world.

In a truth that belies the title of this chapter, it is not really a whole new world that we are called to enter. Christ is not inviting us into a separate Christian fantasy world. The old hymn says: "This world is not my home, I'm just a-passing through,"[6] but the truth is that planet Earth of the twenty-first century is our home. It is God's good creation, and we are put here to do God's work right here and right now. If we understand the nature of our world, we can better complete our faith journey in it.

A World with Good and Evil

Many of the stories that are popular in today's culture—from the films of Woody Allen to the legal thrillers of John Grisham—raise issues of moral ambiguity. Their narratives paint with shades of gray and blur the line between good and evil. There is value in such stories. Looking at the world in black and white is simplistic and can lead us to be judgmental, even to the point of launching crusades against others. But stories that blur the lines between good and evil may also leave readers and viewers with the impression that there is no such thing as right and wrong or good and evil.

Ancient myths and legends speak to humankind's desire to distinguish right from wrong and to take a strong stand for what is right. That is also part of the appeal of today's fantasy stories. They make it clear that good and evil exists in the world, and they show our heroes battling in concrete ways on the side of good and against the forces of evil.

The Harry Potter stories, *Star Wars* films, and *The Lord of the Rings* are all set in a moral universe that presumes the presence of good and evil. As a matter of fact, many have identified the struggle between good and evil as the primary theme of the stories. In all three series, we find a clear force of good in the universe and a dark side that must be resisted.

These stories argue that good and evil are present in the world through the literary strategy of *indirect commentary.* The opposing view—that there is no such thing as good and evil—is put into the mouths of despicable characters. Toward the end of *Harry Potter and the Sorcerer's Stone,* Voldemort's servant explains that Voldemort has talked him out of his "ridiculous ideas about good and evil." He tells Harry, "There is no good and evil, there is only power."[7] In both *The Empire Strikes Back* (1980) and *Return of the Jedi* (1983), Darth Vader tries to downplay the relevance of right and wrong by telling Luke, "You don't know the power of the dark side."

In *The Fellowship of the Ring,*[8] the wizard Gandalf discovers that the wizard Saruman has given up his title "Saruman the White," a title suggesting moral purity, and taken on the title "Saruman of Many Colours." Saruman has traded in his white robes for a robe woven of many-colored threads that can change color whenever he moves. He has become amoral, and is going to use his power only to benefit himself. By claiming that they are beyond petty concepts such as good and evil, Voldemort's servant, Darth

Vader, and Saruman all demonstrate just how corrupted by evil they have become.

Although all three fantasy series assume the presence of evil in the world, they offer different perspectives on the origin and nature of evil. Philosophers and theologians sometimes make a distinction between a Manichaean and an Augustinian view of evil. The Manichaean view of evil takes a dualistic approach to the nature of the universe. Good and evil are in conflict in the world. Evil, as well as good, is an eternal part of the very nature of the universe. The *Star Wars* films seem to be most consistent with this view of evil. The light side and the dark side of the Force are in eternal conflict. In *The Phantom Menace,* Jedi Council member Mace Windu speaks of "the prophecy of the one who will bring balance to the Force." According to this prophecy, the ultimate resolution of this conflict will come not when one side defeats the other, but when the two equal sides of the Force come into balance.

Augustine saw this Manichaean view of evil as heresy. He argued that the origin of all things was a good God. According to the Augustinian view, there is no Evil Creator God that serves as an equal balance to the Good Creator God. Put another way, Satan is not equal with God, but merely a fallen angel. When God created the world, God proclaimed it good. Evil came into the world only as the result of the fall, when people did not follow God's good way. At its core, however, the nature of the universe is ultimately good. *The Lord of the Rings'* approach to the nature of evil seems to have much in common with this view. As Elrond says in *The Fellowship of the Ring:* "[N]othing is evil in the beginning. Even Sauron was not so."[9] The One Ring is not a force in and of itself, but rather must draw the people around it into forsaking the good in their hearts. The Nazgûl, former kings who are corrupted in their desire for power, turn into wraiths and have only a shadow existence as they are consumed with evil.

The Harry Potter stories clearly acknowledge the presence of evil in the world, but so far the books have not articulated a view of the origin or nature of that evil in Harry's world.

Although the views of the nature of evil in today's fantasy stories differ in subtle ways, they all agree on the way evil is confronted and ultimately defeated. This is not simply a confrontation of power against power, and good does not defeat evil by being equal or greater in strength and power. This is illustrated quite graphically in the films of each series. Harry looks like (and is) just a small boy when he confronts Voldemort in *Harry Potter and the Sorcerer's Stone,* and he is much smaller than the basilisk that attacks him in *Harry Potter and the Chamber of Secrets.* Darth Vader towers over Luke Skywalker in the *Star Wars* films and holds a more powerful lightsaber as well. In *The Lord of the Rings,* the Balrog that Gandalf confronts is many times larger than he is, and Frodo and Sam are tiny and weak compared to nearly every menace that they face. In these fantasy stories, victory does not come to those with the most strength or the most power. Instead, evil is defeated through weakness, humility, the love of friends and family, and sacrifice. In other words, good triumphs over evil precisely because it is good.

Many passages in the Bible have been understood to be consistent with the Augustinian view of good and evil. Jesus' teachings in the Gospels assume the presence of both good and evil in the world (Matt. 5:45). But according to the Gospels, Jesus did not teach that good and evil are forces that can be reconciled or held in a balance. According to the Gospel of Matthew, Jesus taught that the kingdom of Satan (who is often called the evil one) is clearly opposed to the Kingdom of God, and that which is evil is diametrically opposed to that which is good (Matt. 12:25–37). Jesus taught his disciples to see their lives as a struggle on the side of righteousness against the forces of evil (Matt. 6:13, John 17:15). But in the Gospels, Jesus does not battle evil as though he were taking part in an eternal battle of power against power. He does not confront evil with conventional strength or power. Instead, he confronts evil with love, forgiveness, and the ultimate sacrifice.

One of the keys to understanding the moral nature of the world of the Bible is to understand that it is a world that is created by a good God. Not all of the gods of ancient myths were good. As a matter of fact, many of the gods in Greek myths were scoundrels who often plotted against the purposes of humankind. In contrast, the biblical narratives assume that God is wholly good—goodness is one of God's essential characteristics. In other words, goodness itself is predicated on the very nature of God (Mark 10:18), and evil occurs when God's will is not done (Gen. 3).

As we go forth in our faith journeys, it is important for us to recognize that we live in a world where both good and evil are present. As we journey, we strive to avoid evil, to do what is good, and to stay true to a good God.

A Miraculous World

Decades ago people of faith had to contend with a culture that prided itself on holding a rational and scientific skepticism toward all things spiritual and supernatural. But times have changed. Today's world is filled with songs, television shows, novels, and films that express a longing for and openness to a spiritual and supernatural world. Harry Potter lives in a world that contains moving paintings, enchanted ceilings, flying broomsticks, invisibility cloaks, screeching letters, and ghosts. In the *Star Wars* universe, Jedi Knights tap into the Force to make things float, anticipate where laser blasts are going to hit, and sense what they cannot see. Glowing swords, magic rings, and wizards conjuring spells are all part of Middle-earth. These things do not have a natural cause or explanation. They are *super*natural.

The Gospels are set in a supernatural world as well. Jesus and the disciples live in a world that is not limited by the rules of science and reason. The world of the Gospels is a world that goes beyond what we can see, analyze, or prove. God can intervene in human history, and miracles can happen. When John the Baptist's disciples ask for evidence that Jesus is indeed the one who has come to usher in a new world, Jesus uses miracles as evidence: "Go and tell John what you have seen and heard: the blind receive their sight, the lame walk, the lepers are cleansed, the deaf hear, the dead are raised, the poor have good news brought to them" (Luke 7:22, Matt. 11:4).

Certainly a supernatural aspect is present in the worlds described in the fantasy stories, but it is also true that life is largely lived by the laws of nature. Magic does not occur in every situation. People generally walk from place to place, and only rarely do they "apparate," magically appear and disappear from place to place. Even great wizards tend to solve problems with their minds and by research; they do not magically know the answer to every question. It is a *super*natural world, but life is most often lived by natural rules.

Through this lens we can look at the biblical world and see that the same principle holds true in the world of the Gospels. Even in the biblical world, there is a restraint of miracles. Yes, Jesus does walk on water (Matt. 14:25–33), but he usually goes by boat. Jesus healed many by miraculous means, but many more who were living at the time of Jesus were healed by medical and natural means. He fed thousands through his miracle with the loaves and fish, but many more who were hungry in Jesus' day were fed through the generosity of others.

This restraint of miracles helps us keep the miraculous nature of our world in perspective. Recognizing that miracles can happen does not mean that we should expect all our problems to be solved magically. It also does not mean that we should look for supernatural explanations for every event that occurs in our life.

It is important to note that there are many contrasts between the miracles of the Bible and the practice of sorcery. First of all, miracles in the Bible are not done through the magical power of an individual, but as a sign of the power of God. Unlike sorcery, miracles are not some learned "craft" that highlights an individual's ability to tap into a hidden power source, but rather are demonstrations of the power of God in the world. According to the Gospels, even the miracles performed by Jesus himself were recognized as the work of the Spirit of God, and people immediately responded to them by giving glory to God (Luke 5:26).

Second, miracles are certainly not the same as sorcery, in which one person holds supernatural power over another through the power of spirits or the occult. Although the Bible assumes the possibility that God can cause miracles, it condemns the practice of sorcery (Exod. 22:18, Deut. 18:9–12, Gal. 5:19–21). Our appreciation of the supernatural aspects of the world should not drive us to attempt to practice sorcery, or even so-called white magic, but rather to recognize and rely on God's power. Conservative and liberal Christian Churches alike warn against both the practical and spiritual dangers of getting involved in groups that practice sorcery or witchcraft, use incantations, or dabble in the occult.[10]

Third, miracles are not identical to the magic performed in these fantasy stories. Jesus did not do magic tricks; he did not conjure visions or make himself fly around. His miracles purposefully demonstrated the power of God and the nature of the Reign of God. Jesus' miracles demonstrated that God has dominion over nature, the demonic, disease, and even death itself. His miracles helped people, and in so doing, they demonstrated God's power to redeem people from the forces that exist in a fallen world. His miracles gave people a glimpse of the way things happen when God rules, when God's will is done on earth as it is in heaven. In other words, they were evidence of the Reign of God on earth.

Finally, recognizing the supernatural dimensions of life should not mean that we become superstitious. Some Christians may be tempted to see signs everywhere or even to try to divine God's will through the flip of a coin. But God is not our Magic 8-ball, allowing us to abdicate responsibility for making tough decisions in our lives. Just because the Bible shows that God can intervene in the world does not mean that God is intervening in every event that occurs in our daily lives. There is a real temptation, even for Christians, to become superstitious rather than faithful.

What, then, are we to make of our miraculous world? Living in a miraculous world challenges us to expand our understanding of what is possible. It calls us to acknowledge that, in the words of William Shakespeare, "There are more things in heaven and earth, Horatio, / Than are dreamt of in your philosophy."[11] We need to recognize that there is more to this world than we can fit into our human understanding. God can create miracles in our lives. In the Harry Potter stories, muggles walk around failing to see the magic that occurs around them, but we have been given eyes to see God's miraculous work in our lives and the lives of those around us.

The disciples saw the power of miracles firsthand, but it did them no good because they failed to recognize its significance for their lives. They saw Jesus feed five thousand people with a few loaves and fish, but a little while later, they were again at a loss to see how Jesus would be able to feed just four thousand people (Mark 6:30–44, 8:1–10). The miracle served as a test for the disciples, to see if they had eyes to see who Jesus truly was. God's revelation of Jesus Christ and God's Reign was the central miracle of God,[12] and the disciples failed to see it. In the Gospel of Mark, even after seeing all Jesus' miracles, the disciples abandoned Jesus when he was arrested. As they sat huddled together after Jesus' crucifixion, the disciples probably did not feel that life was miraculous at all. They probably felt defeated and as though there was no way out. But the disciples would eventually see the miraculous power of God to overcome any obstacle, even the obstacle of death. Although they were not extraordinary people by human measure, God would use these simple disciples to do extraordinary things. The Acts of the Apostles attests that God used these same disciples to turn the world upside down. God was able to work miracles in their lives and through their lives because of their faithfulness.

The key to understanding our miraculous world, then, is to understand the good God who created the world and has chosen to intervene in it. Many people have personal struggles with addiction, depression, or other obstacles, and they feel that it is not humanly possible to find a way out of them. The good news is that a Higher Power exists who can overcome any obstacle. God can work miracles in our lives and through our lives. These miracles might not take the form of the flashy magic of fantasy stories, and they may not take place in an instant. But the world of our faith journey is a world in which all things are possible with God.

Providence: God's Work in the World

Miracles are just one aspect—a clear and dramatic aspect—of a broader and more complex issue in our understanding of the world: that of providence. God's providence, the nature of God's ongoing care of and control over creation, is a complicated and hotly debated doctrine that has challenged the minds of theologians for centuries. A dialogue with these fantasy stories certainly will not answer all the theological questions raised by the concept of providence, but it does allow us to step outside of our world and gain some helpful perspectives on the nature of God's work in the biblical narratives and in the world today.

In *Star Wars: A New Hope,* Han Solo speaks for many viewers when he says, "I've never seen anything to make me believe there's one all-powerful force controlling everything." It is perhaps surprising, in such cynical times, to discover a sense of providence permeating all three of today's popular fantasy series. Though God is not explicitly mentioned in the Harry Potter stories, *Star Wars* films, or *The Lord of the Rings,* a clearly benevolent *purpose* drives certain events in these worlds.

Harry Potter is *meant* to survive and battle Voldemort. In the *Star Wars* films, the Force guides the destinies of Jedi Knights and others. In *The Lord of the Rings,* according to Gandalf and Aragorn, the hand of fate is lurking over many events of the past, present, and future.

Providence is an overarching theme in the Bible as well. Through good times and bad, the Bible repeatedly indicates, both implicitly and explicitly, that God's purpose is being served (Deut. 32:7-43; Ps. 24:1, 74:12–17; Matt. 6:25–33; 1 Pet. 1:3–9).

To say that providence is at work in the worlds of today's fantasy stories, however, does not mean that their narratives play out as though there is a foreordained script and every event simply moves toward its foregone conclusion. In *The Fellowship of the Ring,* when Lady Galadriel shows Sam and Frodo the Mirror of Galadriel, she tells them that it will show them images of "things that were, things that are, and things that yet may be."[13] She explains that whether they are seeing actual future events, or only potential future events that will never come to be, depends on their choices and actions.[14] In the film version of *The Lord of the Rings: The Fellowship of the Rings,* she tells Frodo, "Even the smallest of persons can change the course of the future."

Introducing human agency and free will into the equation adds considerably to the drama in these stories. With human agency comes uncertainty, accidents, and mistakes. Harry Potter and his young friends fumble their way toward thwarting Voldemort and make many mistakes along the way. In the *Star Wars* films, Luke Skywalker, Leia Organa, Han Solo, and Chewbacca rush headlong into and out of trouble. In *The Fellowship of the Ring,* Frodo Baggins and his young friends blunder their way to the Prancing Pony, only to find that Barliman Butterbur has gaffed by failing to deliver Gandalf's letter. Because of the human activity that is part of these stories, these worlds hold uncertainty.

In the same way, although the Bible speaks of God's control over the world, its narratives do not present humans as automatons or events as matters of predestination. God is in control of the big picture, such as when God provides salvation to humankind through Jesus' death and resurrection. When we read the biblical narratives, however, we find that the humans in them are free to be obedient or disobedient. They can and do accomplish great things, but they can also make mistakes. Therein lies the complexity of the doctrine of providence.

In the Bible, God is not a grand puppet master who is moving everything and everyone around a stage. This can be disconcerting for those who are inclined to believe that God intervenes in every detail of their lives by providing them with a convenient open parking place when they are running late for an appointment or by sending a guardian angel to stop them from falling if they slip when they go mountain climbing. At times we may wish for a God who micromanages the world. But on reflection, do we truly wish for such a God or such a world? Audiences of the film *The Truman Show* (1998) cheered when Truman Burbank left his world, because they could not fathom living in a world where the "creator" was determining every aspect of their lives, even if it was an idyllic world created for their own safety and comfort.

Today's fantasy stories do not provide us with profound philosophical answers to the question of providence. They do, however, offer us some interesting visions of providence that can help us to reflect on it.

Harry Potter and the Sorcerer's Stone offers a provocative image of providence on a small scale. The character of Professor Albus Dumbledore, headmaster of Hogwarts School of Witchcraft and Wizardry, is depicted as having some godlike qualities. He is said to be the greatest and most powerful wizard in the world. He is the only person the Evil One, Voldemort, fears. And Dumbledore's moral character is beyond reproach. He does not discriminate, he forgives people, and he gives them second chances. It is repeatedly said of him that he knows everything that happens at Hogwarts. It is interesting, then, to see how he uses, and chooses to restrain from using, his power in his world. At the end of their adventures, Ron Weasley suspects that Dumbledore gave Harry, Ron, and Hermione just enough help, guidance, and resources that they would be able to find Lord Voldemort and face him in mortal combat. Harry's very life is put into danger. Hermione is appalled by that notion. Why on earth would Dumbledore allow them to face such danger and not intervene himself? Harry offers one possibility:

> "He's a funny man, Dumbledore. I think he sort of wanted to give me a chance. I think he knows more or less everything that goes on here, you know. I reckon he had a pretty good idea we were going to try, and instead of stopping us, he just taught us enough to help. . . . It's almost like he thought I had the right to face Voldemort if I could. . . ."[15]

Is this how we picture God? Why does God choose to work through human agency? Why does God leave so many things up to the church instead of intervening directly? One disturbing implication of this vision of providence is that it does not guarantee that we will be protected from harm. In all three of the fantasy stories, those who are wise in the ways of providence and destiny (Professor Dumbledore, Yoda, and Gandalf) make it clear that the heroes are in very real danger and that there is no guarantee that they will succeed in their quests. As a matter of fact, those who are wise are usually the first to warn of great peril ahead. Still, they are also the ones who demonstrate the greatest serenity in the face of danger.

The New Testament does not guarantee that God will prevent bad things from happening to believers either; many passages practically guarantee that they will face hard times. According to the Gospel of Matthew, Jesus tells his disciples that they will suffer trials if they follow him faithfully (Matt. 10:37–39). The New Testament epistles made it clear to the early Church that they would suffer trials and tribulations as well. When these trials and tribulations came, they were to be expected, and were not to throw them into a crisis of faith.

The *Star Wars* films offer us another interesting perspective on providence through their repeated references to the destiny and will of the Force. Even when *Star Wars* characters recognize the hand of providence, they are uncertain of what it means for the future. In *The Phantom Menace* (1999), Qui-Gon Jinn finds Anakin and boldly proclaims, "Finding him was the will of the Force, I have no doubt of that." Still, when pressed by Yoda, Qui-Gon admits, "His fate is uncertain." In *Attack of the Clones* (2002), Yoda says, "Impossible to see, the future is."

How do we reconcile God's providence with the uncertainty that seems to be present in the biblical narratives and our world? Does believing in God's providence mean that we should be able to see what the future has in store? According to the Gospel of Matthew, Jesus said that other than God, no one—not even Jesus himself—would know when the Son of Man would return (Matt. 24:36). But many Christians obsess about signs of the end times, and try to figure out in great detail what is going to happen next. Jesus taught that these signs have been around since the days of Noah, and that our job is simply to always be alert and prepared, come what may (Matt. 24:37–44).

The destiny of the Ring of Power in *The Lord of the Rings* serves as a profound example of providence at work. This One Ring has a complex history. In ancient times it is heroically cut off the finger of Sauron, the Dark Lord, and then it falls off the finger of a corrupted Isildur and is lost for ages. Later it is found by Déagol, stolen by murderous means by Sméagol, and then found (or stolen?) by Bilbo Baggins. Finally, Gandalf pressures Bilbo to pass it on to Frodo. Thus, from a mortal point of view, the Ring has been passed on by heroic deed, accident, luck, evil action, and intention. Still, knowing all this history, Gandalf sees the hand of providence at work. In the film version of *The Lord of the Rings: The Fellowship of the Rings* (2001), he tells Frodo: "There are other forces at work in this world, Frodo, besides the will of evil. Bilbo was meant to find the Ring. In which case, you were also meant to have it. And that is an encouraging thought."[16] Gandalf seems to indicate a benevolent purpose at work in the destiny of the Ring that belied its seemingly erratic history.

From a human point of view, we might look at the erratic history of ancient Israel or the trial and crucifixion of Jesus and fail to see

God's hand at work. Though we may not be able to see a purpose in every detail of the history of ancient Israel or the life of Jesus, through the eyes of faith, we can see a larger purpose at work in the grand events of world history—even those that challenge our belief in God's providence.

We can best understand the nature of providence when we come to understand that the God who created the world can intervene in it, and cares about its ultimate destiny. By beginning our reflection on providence with our understanding of God, we can avoid many of the pitfalls that Christians can fall into when they think about God's work in the world.

If the God of the Bible is a good God, then it does not make sense to hold to a view of providence that makes God out to be a cruel punisher who curses people with terrible diseases or a sadistic teacher who teaches people a lesson by striking them with tragedy. That would go against everything that the Gospels teach us about God.

In Jesus' day many people believed that if someone was sick or had a disease, it must have been because it was God's will. They felt that God must have cursed these people or they would not be afflicted. So those who were sick or had a disease were considered unclean. Jesus responded to this attitude by stretching forth his hand to those in need, touching them, and healing them. His actions gave his followers a glimpse of the Reign of God. When God reigns—when things are done God's way on earth—then people are healthy, not sick. The people Jesus healed were not cursed, but belonged to the Reign of God.

Even today some Christians think that if someone in their family is ill or suffers misfortune, it must be by the providential will of God. They respond to every misfortune by trying to figure out if God is doing this to them to chastise them or to teach them a lesson. The Book of Job, however, suggests to us that bad things do happen to good people, that God does not intervene on behalf of every faithful prayer for healing or protection, and that we should not even expect to be given a reason for why these things happen (see also Ps. 73). Believing that God is bringing about every misfortune for a reason may be comforting in the short term, but it ultimately warps our image of God. If we believe that God made our child sick or caused us to be robbed as a punishment because we were unfaithful, or in order to strengthen our faith because we were not faithful enough, then we turn God into a cruel and vindictive Lord (like Sauron) or a sadistic teacher (like Professor Snape). That approach to providence can cause long-term damage to our relationship with God.

Bad things happen in this fallen world. We do not live in a heaven on earth, where everything that happens is exactly according to God's will. But we are called to respond to this world, in good times and in bad, with faith, hope, and trust in God. Faith in God's providence does not mean that we know all the reasons involved but that we believe that there is reason in the world. It means that our goal is not to try to figure out a specific purpose that God might have for allowing every specific trial, but rather that we believe in a benevolent purpose in the world—despite the evil that happens in it.

What is the exact nature of God's providence in the world? We will not come to an answer here. Many biblical passages teach that we cannot grasp what God's providence means because the nature of God is beyond us (Job 11:7–9, 26:14, 36:26; Eccles. 3:11, 11:5; Isa. 40:28). According to the prophet Isaiah, "'For my thoughts are not your thoughts, nor are your ways my ways,' says the LORD. 'For as the heavens are higher than the earth, so are my ways higher than your ways and my thoughts than your thoughts'" (Isa. 55:8–9). But while we may not understand the details, we can find comfort in knowing that ultimately nothing that happens in this world can separate us from the love of God, which is in Christ Jesus our Lord (Rom. 8:37–39). And that is an encouraging thought indeed.

The key to understanding the world of our faith journey is to understand the good God who created it, who can intervene in it, and who cares about its ultimate destiny. It is into the world of this God that we are called. As fascinating as our world is, however, we are not called into it merely to be passive spectators. Harry Potter gets to see the wonders of Diagon Alley and go to school at Hogwarts, but he also has to take on the task of battling the evil Voldemort. In *Star Wars: A New Hope,* Luke Skywalker gets his wish to see the wider galaxy beyond Tatooine, but he also becomes intimately involved with the Rebellion's struggle for freedom. In *The Lord of the Rings,* Samwise Gamgee fulfills his dream of seeing elves, but his calling takes him far beyond a repast in Rivendell. The next chapter addresses this personal involvement in a cosmic quest: What does it mean when God calls us to embark on a faith journey?

Questions for Reflection

What fantasy world would you most like to visit? Why?

Have you experienced a point in your faith journey when you entered into a wider world? If so, how would you describe that experience?

How is your understanding of the world different from that of those you know who are not believers?

Which fantasy story's view of the world is the most consistent with your own? Which fantasy story's view of the world is the most different from your own?

How do you understand the nature of miracles and the miraculous in our world?

How do you understand the outworking of God's purpose in the world?

What scripture passages have influenced your view of providence the most? What scripture passages do you know of that do not seem to fit easily into your view of providence?

How does your understanding of God's providence help you in your faith journey?

A Call to Journey

When I was serving as a pastor, I had the profound privilege of talking to a number of people, church members and non-church members alike, in the final days and weeks of their lives. When these people talked about their lives, they did not reflect on the success of their careers or the size of house they were able to buy. Instead, almost without fail, they shared with me what they now saw as the most important parts of their lives. They told stories of working with young people in community organizations, teaching children in Sunday school, and how they had learned to accept and forgive another in order to strengthen their relationship with their spouse and children. Some may say that it is only natural that they would speak to me of such things because I was a pastor. That may be true in part. But I often had the distinct impression that they were sharing these things with me because I was one of the few people who would allow them to talk about the fact that their life was coming to an end. I think these men and women were sharing with me the wisdom they had gained from their unique perspective on life. They wanted their lives to count for something. They wanted to leave something behind that would make a difference in the world. Some were sorry that they had seen what was truly important only at the end of their life, when it was too late to leave behind much of a legacy. Others were thankful that they were granted the opportunity to serve God and their neighbors in ways that had a lasting impact.

Throughout the ages people have longed to escape from mundane and meaningless lives. We want our lives to count for something. We want to make a difference in the world. We want to be part of something that is bigger than ourselves. And although we may be embarrassed to admit it, many of us feel that somehow, in some way, we have a great destiny to fulfill. In other words, we sense a calling to live our lives for a higher purpose. It is not surprising, then, that one of the most riveting moments in many legends and myths is the call of the hero to pursue a quest.

Receiving the Call

As the story of Harry Potter begins, Harry is just plain miserable living at number 4 Privet Drive. When the giant Hagrid shows up and delivers an invitation to attend Hogwarts, Harry is at first taken aback, but soon he is thrilled and relieved to receive it. In *Star Wars: A New Hope,* Luke Skywalker is bored with his life on Tatooine. He says that he can't wait for someone to "teleport me off this rock." Still, he is anxious when R2-D2 gives him a cryptic message about Obi-Wan Kenobi, and very hesitant when Obi-Wan calls him to leave Tatooine and join his quest. In *The Hobbit,*[1] Bilbo Baggins seems quite content with his peaceful life in his hobbit hole at Bag End. But when Gandalf calls him out of his happy life and into a wider world of wizards, goblins, and dragons, Bilbo comes to embrace the adventure despite himself.

In each case the normal, everyday life of these characters was interrupted by a call to adventure. While they may have had different levels of contentment in their lives, they were all taken by surprise. They receive a visitation—an epiphany—and their lives would never by the same again.

In the same way, Jesus' disciples were called forth from various lifestyles and, one suspects, various levels of contentment. Simon, Andrew, James, and John were all busy at work in their fishing businesses when a traveling teacher named Jesus came by and said "Follow me, and I will make you fish for people" (Matt. 4:19). According to the Gospel of Matthew, both pairs of brothers immediately left their jobs and their families to follow him (Matt. 4:20, 22). Matthew was sitting in his tax booth, working at a job that made him good money but few friends, when Jesus came by and said, "Follow me." Matthew also got up and followed him (Matt. 9:9).

The twelve, Jesus' hand-selected inner circle of disciples, had most likely heard of Jesus before he came along and called them. But when reading the Gospels, one feels a sense of urgency to this call. The disciples felt this urgency and responded to it immediately. Whether they were content in their lives or were living as malcontents, these twelve and many others through the centuries have dropped everything to follow Jesus.

Today our call to a faith journey comes to us in many different ways, but it often comes to us as a surprise. There is still an urgency to the call. And it still challenges us to stop doing business as usual and follow our destiny.

The term *call* is often used in religious circles to refer to a call to a full-time paid job as a member of the clergy. Though full-time professional ministry is indeed an important vocation, it is a mistake to think that attending a seminary or entering the professional ministry are the only directions to go when a person is called to serve God. The call to full-time ministry is actually made to all Christians and is carried out by living a full life of faith, regardless of the vocation we may have.

Sometimes following our calling requires that we make major life changes, such as changing jobs, schools, or location. Other times it can mean that we stay where we are, but approach our lives in a whole new way. It may mean that we take on a new cause or a new task in life, and that we have to give up some of our free time to do what we were put on earth to do. But whatever the cost involved, the call to a faith journey is a call worth answering.

Whether we are downright miserable like Harry Potter, bored with life like Luke Skywalker, or quite content like Bilbo Baggins, when we follow God's call, our lives will be enriched. Our calling gives us a reason to live and a direction to travel as we go forth on our life's journey.

The Herald

Many ancient stories feature a herald, a mysterious character who calls heroes to their quests. In many myths, heralds are strange, odd-looking characters that are often underestimated by those around them. On first glance they do not look or act as though they are of any significance. As long as they keep to themselves, these heralds are often looked on with amusement or only mild suspicion. Once they start calling people to adventures, however, they are seen as downright dangerous!

The heralds in today's fantasy stories fit this ancient pattern. In *Harry Potter and the Sorcerer's Stone,* a large number of owls attempt to deliver to Harry an invitation to attend school at Hogwarts. Owls are not necessarily considered extraordinary or magical, but they are perceived as odd and somewhat mysterious. Harry's Uncle Vernon prevents Harry from receiving these invitations, and he even takes Harry and his family away from their house to a cabin on an island, in order to escape the owls' deliveries. But while the family is huddled together in a rickety cabin in the midst of a storm, the door suddenly bursts off its hinges to reveal a huge, shaggy, unkempt giant named Rubeus Hagrid. Hagrid delivers Harry's invitation to enter Hogwarts and, in so doing, invites him into the world of wizards. It is ultimately Hagrid, then, who serves as Harry's herald. Hagrid is certainly odd in appearance and manner to Harry's eyes, and is viewed with suspicion and even fear by the Dursleys. But we soon learn that there is more to Hagrid than meets the eye. He is a good friend, a gentle caretaker, and has won the trust of Hogwarts' headmaster, Albus Dumbledore. What is more, we come to learn that he has a certain nobility that is not apparent on first or even second glance.

In *Star Wars: A New Hope,* R2-D2 serves as a herald, calling Obi-Wan Kenobi out of retirement to help Princess Leia. It is Obi-Wan himself, however, who serves as the herald to Luke Skywalker. When Luke hears the name Obi-Wan Kenobi, he asks his Uncle Owen if he might be related to "old Ben," who lives out in the desert. His uncle replies, "That wizard's just a crazy old man," and tells Luke to forget it. In doing this Uncle Owen is trying to protect Luke from getting involved in such foolishness, but viewers soon discover that Ben is one of the best friends Luke could have, and that he is a great Jedi warrior with little time or patience for foolishness.

At the beginning of *The Hobbit,* Bilbo Baggins is standing outside his door when a stranger comes by. "All that the unsuspecting Bilbo saw that morning was an old man with a staff. He had a tall pointed blue hat, a long grey cloak, a silver scarf over which his long white beard hung down below his waist, and immense black boots."[2] When he is properly introduced, Bilbo recognizes the name Gandalf as the wandering wizard who had sent many lads and lasses on adventures in times past. Revealing his own ambivalence toward adventure, he says, "Bless me, life used to be quite inter— I mean, you used to upset things badly in these parts once upon a time."[3] Adventure, to Bilbo, is both interesting and upsetting. The hobbits of Hobbiton enjoy Gandalf's fireworks, but are wary of him as well. In the film *The Lord of the Rings: The Fellowship of the Rings* (2001), we are told that they have officially labeled Gandalf a disturber of the peace. Though Gandalf is a fun-loving wizard who enjoys relaxing with Bilbo and Frodo, readers soon learn that he is much more.

Jesus served as a herald to the disciples, calling them to follow him and enter the Reign of God. When we compare Jesus to the heralds in these fantasy stories, we may be surprised to find that he has much in common with them. We know, for example, that Jesus of Nazareth did not walk around with a halo on his head, and that everyone he met did not immediately recognize him as the Christ, the Son of God. Instead, many people viewed him as just another traveling teacher and wonder worker. To them he may have been an interesting diversion—and later a dangerous radical—but they were not going to give up their lives to follow him. And yet Jesus' disciples all left what they were doing in order to do just that.

Who are the heralds of God's call in our lives today? We are usually not called by some mysterious stranger who travels into town. As a matter of fact, our herald might not be a person at all, but several aspects of our life of faith. It is true that the Spirit of God can speak directly to our hearts, but God also calls us, or at least confirms our calling, through our churches, our ministers, and other people of faith. For many people these heralds—ministers, church community, and even God—are misunderstood and not entirely trustworthy. Friends and family who have accepted our faith quest as an amusing pastime, on a par with Gandalf creating fireworks, may suddenly become suspicious when we start to take its call seriously. My wife, Lisa, had a friend in high school tell her, "I think it's good that you have religion and all, but you shouldn't let it affect your life." When our faith starts to make demands on our lives, others may not understand. They may see our faith as an unwelcome herald that is calling us to leave their world and enter into a strange and even dangerous adventure.

Sometimes the warnings of friends and family should be heeded. For every good Gandalf, there is a Saruman seeking to lead people astray with appealing words. Jesus himself had to warn his disciples about false prophets (Matt. 7:15, Mark 13:22). There are many wolves in sheep's clothing who are either misguided or even intentionally running scams. We would be wise to make sure that those who are guiding us are trustworthy and are part of reputable churches or non-profit organizations before we give them our devotion or our money.

Still, even when we are guided by those in the most reputable of established churches, some people will not understand our devotion to our faith journey. Those who are part of our journey of faith—including the Spirit of God, our churches, our ministers, and other people of faith—are peculiar heralds indeed. But the call is worth answering.

Human, Heroic, Humble, and Up to the Task

Along with wanting their lives to count for something, people also have an inherent desire to know that they are special. This is another motif that is present in ancient myths, legends, and the fantasy stories of today. Heralds are not the only ones who are underestimated in these stories. Heroes are underestimated as well. Their community underestimates them, and they even underestimate themselves. They usually live a normal, mundane life, and fail to recognize just how special they are.

As he grew up on Privet Drive, those closest to him told Harry Potter, in every conceivable way, that he was not worth much. Harry is presented to the reader as the ultimate underdog. He is awkward, his clothes do not fit him well, and he is prone to getting into trouble by causing accidents. He is bullied, mistreated, and dismissed both at home and at school. On his eleventh birthday, however, Harry learns that he is a wizard, and a famous one at that. Even as he doubts his abilities, Hermione affirms him, telling him, "Harry—you're a great wizard, you know."[4] Harry gets the wonderful news that, despite appearances, he is really a very special person indeed.

Bilbo and Frodo Baggins may not have thought that they had much to contribute to their world. Hobbits are quite literally small people, living in their own little corner of Middle-earth, apart from the great happenings of their world. But Gandalf has occasion to tell both of them that there is something quite extraordinary about them.

At times Gandalf himself seems surprised at how exceptional these small hobbits are. As they bravely go forth on their journeys, Bilbo and Frodo come to see for themselves that they are special people indeed, with unique gifts, hidden strengths, and a spirit of adventure that neither knew he had. One of the running motifs of these tales is that these small and humble hobbits come to be recognized, by themselves and by those around them, as the special people that they are.

When Jesus called the twelve apostles, he called a group of people who were not extraordinary by human standards. Most of them were laborers and fishermen from the Galilean countryside. But Jesus called them to his inner circle of disciples, and God eventually used them to change the world.

Jesus made it a point to seek out those who were overlooked by society. He ministered to lepers, those who could not walk, widows, children, Samaritans, Gentiles, tax collectors, and others. He blessed them with his touch and affirmed their faith in front of their communities. These people lived in a world that did not recognize that they were special, but Jesus showed them that in the Reign of God, they were special indeed.

The Christian faith teaches that humans are not forgettable, irrelevant beings, but rather holy people, fearfully and wonderfully made (Ps. 139:14). The Bible teaches us that human beings are created in the image of God (Gen. 1:26), a teaching that affirms the great value and dignity of all human life. This is good reason for both great pride and great humility. People of faith are called on to humbly acknowledge that they are special and capable beings created by God.[5] At the same time, we are called on to humbly acknowledge that everyone else is special as well, and of great worth as creatures of God.

It is this balance that makes Harry Potter and Frodo Baggins such likable and effective heroes. On the one hand, neither one of them has an inferiority complex. When faced with challenges, they do not cower in a corner, protesting with a false and destructive humility that they are not up to the task, but boldly step up to the epic tasks before them. On the other hand, they carry out their tasks in a humble manner, not thinking of themselves more highly than they ought to (cf. Rom. 12:3), and showing respect to those around them.

In *Harry Potter and the Sorcerer's Stone,* Albus Dumbledore felt that it was important for Harry to live with the Dursleys on Privet Drive instead of growing up in a world that idolized him. Perhaps he knew that Harry would need humility in order to complete the tasks before him. At the same time, Dumbledore shows great confidence in

Harry and helps Harry realize how special he is. In *The Lord of the Rings,* one of Frodo's great virtues is his humility. Frodo knows that he is not greater than others, and offers the Ring willingly to those he thinks are more qualified. Yet he still comes to accept that he is up to the task himself.

We are all made in God's image. As such we are special, and with God's aid we are capable of accomplishing whatever God calls us to do. We are up to the task of changing the world!

Resisting and Accepting the Call

Hearing the call can create a crisis in our life. This wonderful opportunity carries with it potentially terrible consequences. Although we are each called to different journeys, our call almost always requires that we leave behind the comfort and security of what is familiar in order to journey into the unknown.

Perhaps because of this, the heroes of ancient legends and myths often initially reject their calling. The same is true in today's fantasy stories. When Hagrid tells Harry that he is a wizard, Harry's first reaction is to say that there must be some mistake. In *Star Wars: A New Hope,* Luke Skywalker initially turns down Obi-Wan's invitation to join the quest. He says: "I've got to go home. . . . I can't get involved! I've got work to do." The ongoing, mundane things of the world almost prevent him from accepting his call. Upon arriving at Rivendell, Frodo Baggins makes it clear that as far as he is concerned, his part of the quest is over. In each case these heroes cannot imagine themselves undertaking the journey to which they are called. But they are mistaken. It is their destiny.

Moses did not immediately accept his calling either. In fact, he tried to wriggle out of it. When God gives him one of the most dramatic callings of all time—through a burning bush—Moses is full of excuses for why he is not the right person for the job and why the task is doomed to failure (Exod. 3–4). He tries to get out of it, but God is persistent and provides Moses with what he needs to fulfill his calling. Jonah also ran away from God's call on his life. It took being tossed off a ship and swallowed by a whale for Jonah to realize that he had to fulfill his calling to go to Nineveh.

Perhaps there is some earthly wisdom in hesitating before rushing headlong into accepting our calling. We must not only accept our calling at the outset, but also have the commitment to keep on the journey even when the going gets tough. According to the Gospel of Luke, Jesus himself said that his disciples should count the cost before becoming his disciples, because to accept the call meant that they would have to show real commitment (Luke 14:25–33). Most quests worth completing require more than a burst of enthusiasm or a desire for a change of pace. When we are open to hearing God's call, we need to be ready to pay the price.

In *The Two Towers*, on the Stairs of Cirith Ungol, Frodo Baggins' friend Samwise Gamgee reflects on the adventure stories he heard as a child. He recalls that he always thought these adventures were things that brave folk went out and looked for because their lives were a bit dull.

> "But that's not the way of it with the tales that really mattered, or the ones that stay in the mind. Folk seem to have been just landed in them, usually—their paths were laid that way, as you put it. But I suspect that they had lots of chances, like us, of turning back, only they didn't. And if they had, we shouldn't know, because they'd have been forgotten."[6]

Sam realized that only those tasks carried on to completion have lasting value. Faith pilgrims often start off with a burst of energy and enthusiasm. But the journey of faith is in many ways more of a marathon than a sprint.

Some who heard Jesus' call rejected him from the start. Others followed him for a while, but then left him. The Gospel of John reports that after hearing some of Jesus' hard teachings, many of his followers turned away. Jesus then asked the twelve if they too wished to go away. Peter answered him, saying: "Lord, to whom can we go? You have the words of eternal life. We have come to believe and know that you are the Holy One of God" (John 6:68–69). They had come to realize that their past lives were not worth living, and they recognized that following Jesus was the one compelling call on their lives.

Christians today are still called to follow Jesus and to live out the will of God for their lives. This call comes to us in many ways, but it still takes courage to accept it. One of the most inspiring scenes in *The Fellowship of the Ring* comes at the moment when Frodo accepts his call. Although Frodo was frightened, and uncertain of all he was getting himself into, he stepped up and said, "I will take the Ring . . . though I do not know the way."[7] The Book of Isaiah tells of a spectacular vision in which God asks, "Whom shall I send, and who will go for us?" (6:8). Although we may not be called in the same way as Isaiah, we are still challenged to respond as he did by saying, "Here am I, send me!" (Isa. 6:8).

A Call to Live Faithfully

When heroes are called to an adventure, they often do not know all the details of the quest they are about to undertake. What they do know is that they are being called to begin a journey into a new world in which they will combat evil. The hero must take that first step into the adventure before he or she learns the details of the quest. To put it another way, heroes must first answer a general call to start the journey before they know the specific path they will be asked to travel.

This is the case in the Harry Potter stories, *Star Wars* films, and *The Lord of the Rings* trilogy. In these stories a herald calls our heroes into a world of adventure. They must find the courage to take a first step into the adventure. Only later are they faced with specific choices for how to act out their calling. Harry Potter, for example, is called to step into the wizarding world, and learns of his family's past battle with evil. It is only later that Harry takes up specific quests to thwart Voldemort. In *Star Wars: A New Hope* Luke takes the step of following Obi-Wan away from his home planet, but it is only later that he falls into his quests of battling the Empire. When Frodo Baggins agrees to leave the Shire in *The Fellowship of the Ring,* he has no idea how far that decision will take him. These heroes are not given a clear idea from the start of what the future holds for them. They do know, however, that their new life has taken on great importance. They also know that in some way they are being called into a struggle between good and evil, and that they are to stand on the side of what is good.

In the same way, Jesus' disciples knew they were leaving their old life behind, but they did not know exactly where they were going when they dropped everything to follow him. The Gospels indicate that Jesus warned the disciples that they would be living as transients, with no regular lodging place (Matt. 8:20) or stable means of support (Luke 9:3). There were a great number of unanswered questions, and it becomes quite clear in the Gospels that the disciples did not know exactly what they were getting into when they accepted Jesus' call. What they did know, however, is that they were following Jesus and his movement. That was enough for them to take that first step in faith.

What is God calling us to do today? This is the central question of a life of faith. Over the years many faithful Christians have worried that somehow they might miss out on God's will for their lives if they are unable to decode some secret message that God has for them. They worry that they might "blow it," and miss their calling. But God's will is not a great mystery or puzzle to those who sincerely seek it. The call to a faith journey is basically the call to live life faithfully. What does God expect from us? Jesus' basic call to his disciples was to follow him and live life for and in the Reign of God. The Book of Micah sums up God's will for people of faith in the following way:

> [God] has told you, O mortal, what is good;
> and what does the Lord require of you
> but to do justice, to love kindness,
> and to walk humbly with your God? (Mic. 6:8)

Most Christians know the basics of how God calls them to live their life: read the Bible, listen to the teachings of their Church, and use their God-given rational minds and common sense. The difficult part for many of us is figuring out how to apply what we know of God's will to our particular circumstances. Even then, many Christians confess that the most difficult part of doing God's will is not figuring out what they are supposed to do but doing what they already know they are supposed to do.

What is God's will for our life? We cannot go wrong if we live our lives striving for justice, being loving and kind, and walking humbly with our God.

What Is Your Quest? Discerning Your Mission in Life

Within the context of the general call to live a faithful life, many people of faith have also heard a specific call upon their lives. Some have referred to this as their mission in life and have come to understand it as the special reason God put them on Earth. Others have felt called to undertake several causes over the course of their lives. God may be calling us to undertake many great quests. These include specific tasks such as feeding the hungry, raising a family, supporting education, working with youth, teaching Sunday school, raising or giving money to support good ministries, building homes for those who do not have adequate housing, or working for peace and justice through political and social action. But how do we determine which quests we are called to undertake?

We do not have Jesus around in person to tell us the details of our calling, as the twelve disciples did. Still, God continues to give us guidance to discern our calling. God calls us to mission through the Holy Spirit, of course. But God also guides us and confirms our calling through other means. Many Christians report that they come to understand their specific mission in life through a gradual process that seems to follow a pattern. First, they discern the needs of the world around them, and find themselves plopped down in the middle of a problem that calls for a solution. Second, they find that the Holy Spirit is moving them to care about solving the problem. Third, they recognize that they have been given gifts and abilities that can help. Finally, other people in the Church affirm their ability to take up the quest.

Today's fantasy stories can help to illustrate this process of discerning a call. Harry Potter, Ron, and Hermione do not go to Hogwarts looking to battle Voldemort. But when they discover that their school and their world are in trouble, they realize that they are the only ones who are able and willing to confront the problem. With Hermione's intelligence, Ron's courage, and Harry's wizarding skill, they set out to accomplish their task. Harry, especially, is affirmed by the headmaster, Albus Dumbledore, and by his friends, who express their confidence in Harry.

In *Star Wars: A New Hope,* young Luke Skywalker wants to leave Tatooine as soon as possible, and in his heart he really wants to help the princess. Because of his loyalty and responsibility to his uncle and aunt, however, Luke cannot accept Obi-Wan Kenobi's invitation to leave Tatooine and save the princess from danger. It is only when his circumstances change, and his aunt and uncle are tragically killed, that Luke accepts the call to go with Obi-Wan. After leaving his past behind, Luke suddenly finds himself in the middle of a rebellion. He believes in the cause of the Rebellion: the Death Star must be destroyed. Luke realizes that he has abilities that can help the cause. He knows that he was skilled at piloting his land cruiser on Tatooine, and what is more, he discovers that he is strong with this mysterious thing called the Force. His friends and fellow pilots invite him to join them in their battle, and in the dramatic climax, Obi-Wan affirms Luke's ability to use the Force.

In *The Fellowship of the Ring,* Frodo Baggins does not seem to have much in the way of talent or abilities to help in a worldwide battle between good and evil. He is not a great warrior, he is not incredibly strong, and he does not possess magical abilities. He even admits that he is frightened to be entering the wider world of Middle-earth. He tells Gandalf that he is not made for perilous quests, and asks why he was chosen for this task. Gandalf replies: "You may be sure that it was not for any merit that others do not possess: not for power or wisdom at any rate. But you have been chosen, and you must therefore use such strength and heart and wits that you have."[8] Only through his circumstances does his destiny become clear. As time goes by, those around him realize that Frodo does indeed have the special gifts and character necessary for his task. As Elrond tells him, "I think that this task is appointed for you, Frodo; and that if you do not find a way, no one will."[9]

How might this pattern play itself out in our lives today? When I was a pastor, a woman in my congregation said she would never have pictured herself as a youth leader. But she recognized that our youth group needed someone with her gifts and abilities, and God had moved her to care about the young people. I assured her, along with others in our youth ministry, that she would be a wonderful addition to our team. She became a real blessing to the members of the youth group, and the ministry was a real blessing to her life as well. At the same time, another woman was excited about our youth ministry and said that she wanted to be a youth leader. Her gifts and personality, however, were not a good fit for the youth group. In that instance God worked through members of the church to help her realize that her gifts were better used in another ministry. She agreed, and was happy to find an area of ministry where she could be of greater service.

What do we do when we are not certain what mission or quest we are being called to undertake? Our desire to know God's will for us should not lead us into a superstitious search for signs. An example of this approach can be found in the all-too-common practice of "putting out a fleece," that is, setting up some sort of test for God. Those who carry out such a practice believe that if God miraculously causes an unusual event to happen, then they will know that they are supposed to choose a certain option for their lives. The practice is based on a passage from the Book of Judges. God calls Gideon to the mission of delivering Israel. Instead of accepting God's clear revelation, Gideon questions it. He concocts a test for God. He lays down a fleece of wool on the threshing floor, and tells God that if there is dew on the fleece alone, but the ground is dry, then he would know that God would deliver Israel by his hand, "as you have said" (Judg. 6:37). God obliges despite Gideon's lack of faith. But Gideon is still not satisfied, and asks God to complete another test, by making the whole ground dewy and keeping the fleece dry (Judg. 6:39–40). Gideon's request for a sign is not an act of faith but rather a demonstration of a lack of faith. It was already clear to Gideon what he was supposed to do. The fact that God accommodated Gideon in this extraordinary case—so extraordinary that it found its way into the Bible—should not lead us to test God as well.

A better approach may be to hear God's calling and use our God-given common sense, based on what we already know of God's will. A number of years ago at a mission conference, a college student was wrestling with her calling. She saw a mission in need, knew the mission was good and right, was moved by the Spirit of God, recognized her own ability and willingness to help, was affirmed by other Christians, and then simply knew what she was supposed to do. She knew that it was within God's will for her life to serve as a missionary for at least a short time, and she certainly knew that it was not contrary to God's will. So she got up in front of the entire conference of hundreds of people and said, "Well, I figure you can't get in trouble for doing what you know is right." She did not need a giant to burst through the door, a droid to give her a secret holographic message, or to inherit a magic ring to hear her calling.

Sometimes we are called to respond to circumstances for which we do not ask. In the film *The Lord of the Rings: The Fellowship of the Ring*, in a section of dialogue that is repeated for emphasis, Frodo says to Gandalf: "I wish the Ring had never come to me. I wish none of this had ever happened." Gandalf replies: "So do all who live to see such times. But that is not for them to decide. All we have to decide is what to do with the time that is given to us."[10]

In the Book of Esther in the Bible, a Jewish girl named Esther becomes the queen of Persia. When Esther's friend Mordecai uncovers a plot to kill Jewish people in the land, he asks Esther to risk her life to save them. Esther probably wished that she had not been called to respond to those circumstances, but Mordecai tells Esther, "Who knows? Perhaps you have come to royal dignity for just such a time as this" (Esther 4:14). According to the Gospel of Luke, before his crucifixion Jesus asked God, "Father, if you are willing, remove this cup from me; yet not my will but yours be done" (Luke 22:42). Jesus did not ask for the task before him, but he responded to it with faith.

We do not always choose our circumstances, but it is up to us to choose how to respond to them. Some people of faith are given a passion for a certain ministry, such as organizing a food pantry in their local church. They may never have asked for the responsibility of starting a local outreach ministry, but the Spirit of God might lay it as a burden on their hearts. They see the need, recognize their own ability to do it, and find that others affirm their ability. Many Christians would never ask to give up free time on evenings and weekends so they can volunteer their time to serve in ministries in their church or community. But life's circumstances find them called to do just that, and they faithfully accept the calling.

Sometimes we are called to make radical changes in our lives. I know of a Christian couple who never would have chosen to raise a child that was not their own. But life's complex circumstances created a situation in which a child needed a family, and they recognized that they had the abilities and resources necessary to make a difference. God called them, and others affirmed that calling for them. They now see raising that child as one of the reasons God put them on the earth. Christians such as Martin Luther King Jr. and Archbishop Oscar Romero were called by God to take stands that they knew would put their lives in jeopardy. They were called to respond to the injustice of their times by giving up their lives, literally, for the sake of the Gospel.

Those around us may not understand this faith of ours that heralds us to a new way of life. It calls us to leave behind the mundane and to live a life of meaning and purpose. Along with this call comes the blessing of knowing that we are special in God's eyes, and that with God's help, we will be capable of carrying out the tasks before us. But the call comes with a price. It is no small matter to accept it. We are called to be faithful in all that we do, but we are often called to specific missions or quests as well. Being called to a faith journey is both a privilege and a responsibility. May we have the courage and wisdom necessary to accept God's call on our lives.

Questions for Reflection

Which fantasy-story herald would you most like to meet, and why?

Who or what has served as a herald to your calling?

Has anyone been suspicious or concerned about the time and commitment you have put into your faith journey? Has anyone ever been suspicious of your church or religious life?

Each fantasy story has a number of characters who are surprised to find that they are indeed special. Which character or incident in the stories most reminded you of yourself or of events in your own life story?

How can we acknowledge that we are special and still be humble?

How do you balance the understanding that you are special, and that everyone else is special as well?

We all have special challenges and joys in carrying out our quests. Which fantasy-story character do you identify with most in their efforts to fulfill their quest?

Have you ever resisted God's call on your life? Has anyone else ever challenged it?

What do you feel are some of your primary quests in life? For what purposes is God calling you to live out your life? Have others affirmed your calling?

Learning the Way: Education and Training for the Journey

When I was a pastor working with a youth group in a northern suburb of Detroit, I tried to teach our teenagers about Christian perspectives on poverty. We looked at Bible passages from the Gospels and the Prophets and even studied some well-known Christian social ethicists. Although the youth group was learning *about* Christian perspectives on poverty, I was discouraged to find that it was not affecting their attitudes toward poverty. It was not until our youth group started to go on Saturdays to distribute clothes at a soup kitchen in downtown Detroit that I began to see some changes take place. By actually meeting people who were struggling financially, and by working with other Christians from around the Detroit area, our young people's head knowledge became heart knowledge. While their ultimate views of the proper political solutions to the problem of poverty may or may not have changed, their ways of thinking about the problem had definitely changed. It was through meeting people at the soup kitchen, as well as studying the Bible and theology books back at church, that they received their Christian education.

The Value of Education

In many ancient legends and myths, the hero's journey is the story of the hero's spiritual education. Through travels and adventures, heroes learn about their world and about themselves. In fact, many ancient stories feature education as a key part of the plot. Heroes often prepare for their quest by being trained by a wise mentor, or they pause during their quest to be trained in the skills necessary to complete the quest. In contrast, other heroes rush into the task ill prepared and then must learn from the school of hard knocks.

Education and training are key features of today's fantasy stories as well. The Harry Potter stories are built around the education of Harry and his friends at Hogwarts. They learn about wizardry, but they are also learning about the way the wizarding world works, about people, about values, and about themselves. In *The Phantom Menace,* Qui-Gon Jinn's final thoughts are of Anakin Skywalker's need for education. His urgent dying words to Obi-Wan Kenobi are: "Promise me you will train him. He is the Chosen One. He will bring balance. Train him." Even with all of Anakin's power and gifts, Qui-Gon knows that he must be trained. In the following episode, *Attack of the Clones,* it is a sign of Anakin's arrogance and a portent of danger ahead that he does not realize he still has much more to learn. Though *The Lord of the Rings* does not contain many passages that refer directly to formal education, it is clear that learning tales and studying scrolls are highly valued in Middle-earth.

Education and training were also key features in the faith journey of Jesus' disciples. The disciples often referred to Jesus as *Rabbi,* a term of respect that literally means "teacher," and took on the role of *disciple,* which literally means "learner." Jesus taught his disciples by his words and deeds and charged his disciples to teach others in turn (Matt. 28:20).

Education is a journey that can take us to new places and provide us with new insights. At its best, education not only informs us but also forms us and transforms us. It is an essential part of our spiritual life.

The Special Nature of Religious Education

In a key sequence in *The Empire Strikes Back,* Yoda trains Luke Skywalker in the swamps of Dagobah. Luke finds Yoda's teaching methods quite frustrating. Yoda often seems to speak in riddles, and asks questions more often than he provides information. It seems as though Yoda is less interested in transmitting data into Luke's brain than he is in teaching Luke a whole new way to think about and approach life.

The Gospels portray Jesus in a similar vein, as a wisdom teacher or a sage. Jesus did not spout off long, abstract lectures on doctrine or moral principles. Instead, he told strange and surprising stories that turned people's assumptions upside down. His parables featured the despised Samaritans as heroes and the respected Pharisees as hypocrites. He also spoke in short and pithy wisdom sayings that often took the form of paradoxes, such as the "first will be last, and the last will be first" (Matt. 19:30) or "For those who want to save their life will lose it, and those who lose their life for my sake will save it" (Luke 9:24). These paradoxes were more likely to make people ponder life than would a list of doctrines or facts. Jesus' actions challenged people's thinking as much as his words did, such as when he healed people on the Sabbath (Mark 3:1–6) or threw over the tables of the money changers in the temple (Mark 11:15–19). Jesus was not interested in just providing his disciples with simple answers. Rather, he wanted them to question their assumptions about the world and start to think about life in a whole new way.

The Bible is not simply a collection of theological essays or a list of abstract doctrines and ethical principles. It does not come to us as a handy answer book with clear-cut answers to frequently asked questions. Instead, the Bible has been revealed to us as historical narratives, stories, poems, prayers, songs, and letters written to specific communities in specific circumstances. Christian educators sometimes treat the Bible as though they think that the writers who wrote it or the Spirit who inspired it made some terrible mistake. They seem to believe that they must fix a Bible story or psalm by decoding it into a theological doctrine or ethical principle. They try to reduce Bible passages to one or two handy points for their students to apply to their lives. But the Bible is so much richer than that. The narrative and poetic nature of the Bible is not a mistake, but a generous gift from God. Each Bible passage provides learners with wonderfully rich nuances—if only teachers would allow their students to explore it without the goal of reducing the passage to just one lesson or sound bite. Through the genres of the Bible, the Spirit of God can speak to people in many ways, on many different levels, and to many different life situations.

In *Harry Potter and the Order of the Phoenix,* Professor Umbridge is more interested in passing on the content of a pre-approved curriculum than in teaching any practical knowledge. Besides being "desperately dull,"[1] her lessons do little to inspire her students or to prepare them for life in "the real world."[2]

The goal of Christian education programs is not just to teach interesting thoughts *about* the Christian faith, but rather to help learners learn how to think as Christians and prepare them to live their lives as Christians. Because religious education deals with the ultimate issues of the universe that philosophers and theologians have debated for centuries, we should avoid teaching any pat answers to these ultimate questions. If someone says that they have a short answer to a question that theologians or Bible scholars have debated for centuries, they are usually being naïve or are simply wrong. If there were easy answers to theological questions such as the nature of the Trinity or the incarnation, they would have been discovered and agreed on years ago. Because the goal of Christian education is to make disciples, we should make sure that our programs deal not only with doctrines, but also with practical ways that we can live out our faith in the real world.

Learning in the Classroom

When most people think about education, they think about a formal education setting in a classroom with a teacher. The Harry Potter stories capture the wonder of going off to school, getting books, entering new classes with new teachers, worrying about tests, learning new information, and gaining new skills. Harry, Hermione, and Ron's ability to solve the mysteries they face is often a direct result of their studies in class and in the library. In *Harry Potter and the Sorcerer's Stone,* Harry, Ron, and Hermione are trapped by the Devil's Snare plant. While Ron is panicking, Hermione calmly recalls the characteristics of the plant, and therefore is able to figure out a way for them to escape. It is indeed a good thing that Hermione pays attention in Herbology class. By contrast, in *Harry Potter and the Order of the Phoenix,* Harry's failure to learn Occlumancy has grave consequences. What some students may dismiss as abstract and irrelevant information can prove quite valuable in real-life situations.

People in first-century Galilee traveled for miles to hear Jesus teach, and the Gospels indicate that he spent a good deal of time teaching his disciples. The Apostle Paul also had an excellent education. Before his conversion on the road to Damascus, he was prepared for his ministry through his education by Gamaliel, a renowned teacher of the Torah.

Do we value our religious education in the same way? Do we engage our formal Christian education with the same enthusiasm that we feel when we read about Harry Potter's classes? Our churches can create religious education experiences for children, teens, and adults that are every bit as engaging as the courses at Hogwarts. Harry's classes were not just facts and reflections about wizardry; they were learning how to *be* wizards. In the same way, Christian education can teach people not only facts *about* Christianity but how to *be* Christians. Christians who actively seek education for their faith journeys have many options before them. They can become actively involved in Sunday school classes, Bible studies, lay institutes, and even seminary courses. All these options can help us on our way.

It is dangerous, however, for us to value knowledge for its own sake. In *Harry Potter and the Chamber of Secrets,* Albus Dumbledore tells Harry that Voldemort was probably the most brilliant student that Hogwarts had ever seen. As admirable as Hermione's study habits are, she knows that some things are more important. When Harry suggests that she is the better wizard because of her academic abilities, Hermione responds: "Books! And cleverness! There are more important things—friendship and bravery . . ."[3] In the same way, in *The Lord of the Rings,* Saruman was the most brilliant and talented of all wizards. But in his character he was not up to his calling to be a guardian of Middle-earth. Knowledge alone does not make us good people.

Often, in order to fulfill our calling, we must pursue and value secular education as well. The Bible provides examples of people who were ardent students of secular training, including the Apostle Paul, who studied Greek poetry and philosophy (Acts 17:16–34), and Shadrach, Meshach, and Abednego, who became top students in Nebuchadnezzar's court, learning the literature and language of the Chaldeans (Dan. 1). Their commitment to learning prepared them to be used by God. A commitment to religious education does not mean that we can ignore other education. Sometimes this education is necessary to fulfill our ultimate calling in life.

Learning from Reading and Research

We might not expect library research to be the stuff of exciting, action-filled stories, but it plays an important role in today's fantasy stories. Hermione is constantly dragging Harry and Ron to the library for after-hours research. In *Attack of the Clones,* Obi-Wan Kenobi goes to a library to research the location of a star system. And in *The Fellowship of the Ring,* even Gandalf needs to leave Frodo to go to a library of sorts to look up scrolls and do research on the One Ring.

Today we are faced with an extraordinary number of books, videos, and Web sites to help us study the Bible, theology, and issues of spiritual growth. This plethora of material provides many opportunities, but with those opportunities comes the responsibility of sorting through the many viewpoints that are offered. By seeking guidance on what to read from people we trust, we can find good, balanced approaches to important spiritual issues. By reading several books on a topic that are written from different perspectives, we discover that no one author has all the answers. That in and of itself is part of our education.

Learning from Experience

In *Harry Potter and the Order of the Phoenix,* Harry's friends ask him to teach them, based on his battles with Voldemort. They find that they can learn more from his real-life experiences than they could in a classroom alone. In *The Lord of the Rings,* Merry and Pippin often seem to be thrown in over their heads, but to their credit, they grow and learn from their mistakes and successes along the way. These pilgrims learn by action and reflection.

Formal education and training for our faith journey is important, but we also need to gain practical experience along the way. Before rushing into a leadership role as the director of a soup kitchen, for example, one would be well advised to volunteer at another soup kitchen and shadow those who run it for a while. Before rushing off to seminary to be a pastor, one would be advised to spend time as a lay leader in a congregation, taking part in worship services, teaching Sunday school, going on missions, and perhaps even going with a pastor on hospital visitations. Practical experience not only helps us sort out our calling, it also makes formal education that much more valuable when we do pursue it.

Learning in and from Community

In *Star Wars: A New Hope,* Han Solo was not convinced by fancy speeches or sermons about the cause of the Rebellion or the Force. They actually seemed to make him all the more skeptical. But by being around people with a belief in something beyond themselves, people who are willing to die for a cause, Han is changed. He becomes a part of the community and starts to share the values and beliefs of the group, even to the point that he tells Luke, "May the Force be with you." Han learns by becoming part of a community.

In his wisdom Jesus established the Church as a community for us to learn with and from. In the Book of Acts, we read that the early Church "devoted themselves to the apostles' teaching and fellowship, to the breaking of bread and the prayers" (Acts 2:42). In many ways the Christian faith is better caught than taught; we learn to be Christians by worshiping, praying, and serving with other Christians. In religious education, this process has been called enculturation. We prepare best for our faith journey by being an active part of a faith community.

Learning from Mentors

Mentor was the name of Odysseus's trusted counselor in Homer's epic the *Odyssey.* Today a mentor is understood to be a wise and trusted counselor or teacher who guides us in our lives. We learn from watching, listening, and working alongside a mentor. These relationships can take many forms.

In the *Star Wars* universe, young Jedi Knights are mentored by older, more experienced Jedi. They wear short hair and a long braid as a sign that they are Padawan apprentices. An apprentice was not meant to become identical to his mentor, nor share the same personality. Qui-Gon Jinn, for example, tended to be adventurous and to take his own initiative. In contrast, his apprentice Obi-Wan Kenobi, at least in his younger days, was more inclined to follow orders from the Jedi Council.

Jesus was a mentor to his twelve disciples. The Gospel of John tells of one of the last lessons Jesus taught his disciples before his crucifixion. Before celebrating the Passover meal, Jesus, who presumably would have been the most honored of all those present, took on the role of a servant and washed his disciples' feet. When he had finished, he told them: "For I have set you an example, that you also should do as I have done to you. Very truly, I tell you, servants are not greater than their master, nor are messengers greater than the one who sent them. If you know these things, you are blessed if you do them" (John 13:15–17). Jesus was serving as the ultimate mentor, teaching by word and example.

Mentoring can be a vital part of any religious education program. We can take the initiative ourselves to find people that we admire, and ask them to talk with us and teach us from their experience. We can go with them as they live out their calling.

We must choose mentors carefully. In *Attack of the Clones,* when Anakin complains about his mentor Obi-Wan, Padmé Naberrie tells Anakin that all mentors have a way of seeing our faults more than we would like. Instead of following Obi-Wan's guidance, however, Anakin listens to Supreme Chancellor Palpatine, who flatters him and plots to use his power. Sometimes better for us to listen to and model the one that does not always say what we want to hear.

Having a personal learning relationship with a mentor is much different than following a nationally known celebrity as though she or he were a guru of the faith. Christians are not to give full allegiance to any human, but to Christ. Jesus warned his disciples that false prophets and teachers would lead them astray.

Even well-intentioned mentors are not perfect. In *Harry Potter and the Order of the Phoenix,* Harry learns that even his beloved godfather is not always the best role model and does not always give him the best advice. Still, watching and learning from a person who is further down the path than we are can be an important part of our religious education.

Receiving a call to embark on a faith journey does not mean that we leave our education behind us. On the contrary, it means that our religious education is even more important because it prepares us for the journey. We can learn from a variety of classes and study groups, by reading and research, through experience and reflection, by living out our faith with others in a community, from mentors, and more. Our education is an important part of our lifelong faith journey.

A Call to Teach?

Before moving on, it seems appropriate to pause and reflect on the call to teach. The vocation of teaching is lifted up and held in esteem in today's fantasy stories. In the Harry Potter stories, we learn that Albus Dumbledore could be the Minister of Magic in charge of the whole wizarding world if he wished, but instead he chooses to be the headmaster of a school. Likewise, in *Attack of the Clones,* Master Yoda is held up as perhaps the greatest of the Jedi. Yet we see him spending his time teaching young children in the way of the Jedi. For Yoda this is a vocation of the highest importance. Most significantly for Christians, of course, is the example of Jesus Christ, who took on the role of a teacher. Education and teaching are lifted up in these stories because on some level we know they are important. Teachers may not receive the highest salary or the highest esteem in our society, but through the eyes of faith, we recognize that teaching is indeed a noble calling.

Even if we are not called to teaching as our full-time vocation, we may be called to teach in a Sunday school, Bible study, or tutoring program. If formal teaching is not our calling, we may be called to mentor those who are younger in the faith than we are. We can volunteer at our church or at a Big Brother and Big Sister program. Sometimes young men and women can learn a great deal just by having the opportunity to tag along with us as we go about our errands and service to our Church and community on a given Saturday. They can learn from us while we learn from them, as we move forward in our faith journeys.

Questions for Reflection

What is your favorite learning moment from the fantasy stories? What do you feel was the most important lesson that someone learned?

How can you improve your Christian education? What books could you read or what classes might you attend? Is there someone you could ask who might recommend books or classes to you?

We often learn by doing. What mission and outreach activities sponsored by your church, your denomination, or another local church or organization could you join?

Are you an active part of a community of faith? How are you learning to be a person of faith by being around other people of faith?

Who are the people of faith that you know and admire the most? Could you ask one of them to consider mentoring you in living as a person of faith?

Have you ever considered being a teacher or a mentor? How could this role be a part of your calling?

Travel Provisions: God Gives Us What We Need for the Journey

Religious jewelry has become increasingly popular in recent years. Some Christians wear crosses on necklaces, the symbol of a fish on a ring, or the letters WWJD engraved into a bracelet. For some people these items are an outward expression of their faith. Others find that wearing religious jewelry serves as an ever-present reminder and helps them reflect on their faith. Sometimes, however, Christians slip from religious reflection into superstition. They wear pieces of religious jewelry as though they were magic amulets or lucky rabbits' feet. They believe that by wearing a cross on a necklace, they will somehow be protected from physical or spiritual danger. But this is the stuff of fantasy, not of religion. To trust in a physical object rather than the immortal and invisible God is idolatry. The special provisions that we are given may be less tangible, but they are still very real.

Myths and legends are filled with stories of magic talismans and amulets. Though the Bible does not condone the use of these, it does use vivid imagery for the provisions that Christians *are* given. The Pauline epistles use metaphors of gifts, fruit, and armor to describe the ways that God provides for us.

Gifts

Part of the magic of ancient stories is in the special gifts and abilities that the hero receives by supernatural means. Depending on the version of the legend that is told, King Arthur received his magic sword, Excalibur, either as a gift from the Lady of the Lake or by pulling it from an enchanted stone. In either case it was a supernatural gift that both facilitated and validated his quest.

Today's fantasy stories also feature special gifts that help the heroes complete their tasks. The special gifts that Harry Potter receives, such as the invisibility cloak from his father, the Marauder's Map from Fred and George Weasley, and his Nimbus 2000 and Firebolt from other adults, are indispensable tools that help him complete his missions. In the *Star Wars* universe, Luke Skywalker receives his father's lightsaber and also has a special gift for being able to draw on the power of the Force. These are essential provisions for Luke's quest. In *The Fellowship of the Ring,* Bilbo gives Frodo the Ring, a valuable dwarf mail shirt to protect him, and his sword, Sting. Later, the Lady Galadriel gives him special life-giving *lembas* bread and a small crystal phial containing the light of Eärendil's Star. All these gifts come into play at key moments in Frodo's journey. If it were not for the gifts they received, the heroes would never succeed on their journeys.

The gift of the Holy Spirit of God is the greatest gift that Christians receive. Jesus promised that after his death, he would not leave his disciples alone; the Holy Spirit would come and empower them to fulfill their calling. He told his followers, "But you will receive power when the Holy Spirit has come upon you; and you will be my witnesses in Jerusalem, in all Judea and Samaria, and to the ends of the earth" (Acts 1:8).

The Apostle Paul wrote that Christians are each given spiritual gifts to help them fulfill their calling and destiny. These spiritual gifts are not merely natural talents, such as singing or athletic prowess. Spiritual gifts, as their name suggests, are both spiritual in nature and gifts from the Holy Spirit of God. In other words, they come from the Spirit and are given by God's grace, and not because the one who receives them is somehow more worthy than others. Paul wrote that these gifts vary from person to person, and include prophecy, ministry, teaching, exhortation, generosity, cheerfulness, leadership, and the speaking in and interpretation of tongues (Rom. 12:3–8, 1 Cor. 12:1–11).

Because the lists of spiritual gifts in Romans, chapter 12, and 1 Corinthians, chapter 12, are not identical, it would be a mistake to consider either of these passages an exhaustive list or a comprehensive explanation of the nature of these gifts. Paul explained to the church of Corinth that these gifts were given to build up the whole Church, not just the individual to whom the gift has been given (1 Cor. 12:7). In this way spiritual gifts are not so much God's gifts to individuals as they are God's gift to the Church as a whole. Paul also explained that just as a human body needs all its various parts, so the body of Christ needs all kinds of people with all kinds of gifts in order to function properly (1 Cor. 12:12–26).

One way we can discern our own spiritual gifts is by prayerfully reflecting on how we have been used to build up the Church and other people. We can ask other Christians what gifts they might recognize in us. How do they see God using us? What gifts of the Spirit do they recognize in our lives? The process of discerning our gifts has some other benefits as well. It helps us better understand our calling, because when we know how God has gifted us, we may have a better idea of how God might use us. Taking time to discern our gifts also helps us to pause and give thanks to God for the gifts that we have been given.

Fruit

In *The Lord of the Rings,* in the midst of a frightening and sometimes violent struggle for survival, Frodo Baggins and Samwise Gamgee have to deal with Gollum, one of the most annoying, dangerous, and repulsive creatures in all of Middle-earth. But the patience, gentleness, kindness, and self-control that Frodo and Sam show to Gollum prove to be among the most powerful tools used to fulfill their quest to destroy the Ring. It is only because they embody these characteristics that they are successful.

Although the gifts of the Spirit are particular to each believer, the Epistle to the Galatians tells us that the fruits of the Spirit are given to every Christian. In contrast to the works of the flesh, "the fruit of the Spirit is love, joy, peace, patience, kindness, generosity, faithfulness, gentleness, and self-control" (Gal. 5:22–23). These fruits of the Spirit do not sound like the weapons of war often described in legends, myths, and fantasy stories. They are strange provisions for a strange quest indeed. If, however, our mission is to bring God's love to earth as it is in heaven, then these fruits may prove more powerful than any sword. We read that Jesus said, "[A]ll who take the sword will perish by the sword" (Matt. 26:52), and we know that Jesus Christ himself won his battle with evil through love, generosity, faithfulness, and self-control.

Armor

In *Harry Potter and the Sorcerer's Stone,* we learn that perhaps the greatest gift Harry Potter received was invisible even to him. He had special protection against the powers of darkness because he had been marked by his mother's gift of sacrificial love. As Dumbledore tells Harry, "To have been loved so deeply, even though the person who loved us is gone, will give us some protection forever."[1]

Living out the fruits of the Spirit may seem to leave us vulnerable. By most accounts, trying to exhibit gentleness and kindness in the midst of battle seems like a good way to get clobbered! But according to Ephesians, God does not leave Christians unprotected. Paul encourages Christians to "take up the whole armor of God, so that you may be able to withstand on that evil day, and having done everything, to stand firm" (6:13). These pieces of armor include the belt of truth, breastplate of righteousness, shield of faith, helmet of salvation, and sword of the Spirit, which is the word of God (Eph. 6:14–17). Some Christians, especially those who are going through challenging spiritual trials, have found it helpful to read this passage each morning, and to envision clothing themselves in this armor. By staying immersed in thoughts of God and the ways of God, they are protected from the temptations that come their way.

Other Talents and Resources

The heroes of fantasy stories use the special gifts and powers they have been given, but they also make use of their own natural talents in order to successfully complete their missions. In *Harry Potter and the Sorcerer's Stone,* Hermione uses her sharp intellect, Harry uses his athletic skill, and Ron uses his skill at playing chess to complete their quest for the stone. These are not magical gifts, but they are important provisions just the same.

The New Testament does not list being a brilliant student, a talented athlete, or adept at planning and strategizing as spiritual gifts. But these God-given talents and others can and should be nurtured and used for God's purpose, and not for selfish gain.

Physical resources can help the cause of good as well. In *The Fellowship of the Ring,* Barliman Butterbur, the innkeeper of the Prancing Pony, provided Frodo, Sam, Merry, and Pippin with lodging and a pony for their journey. There was nothing supernatural about these gifts, but they were a great help to the hobbits in their quest. Barliman was not called to go on the hobbits' mission himself, but in his own small way, he contributed to their mission by giving them what he had to offer.

What resources do we have for the journey? Most of us have a great deal to offer. We have apartments, homes, automobiles, entertainment systems, money, and more. Through the eyes of faith, we recognize that all good gifts come from God, and we are called to be stewards of these gifts and use them for God's purposes. When I was in seminary, my roommates and I used our modest off-campus cabin as a retreat house of sorts for fellow students who needed a break from campus life. It meant cleaning up our messy cabin, and then cleaning it up again when our guests left, but we saw it as a small way that we could practice hospitality and use our home as a ministry. A mother of small children in my church did not have much time to offer for other ministries. She did have a van, however, which she saw quite literally as a godsend. So she made her van available to our youth ministry whenever she could. Many Christians also make use of their money by tithing 10 percent of their earnings to their churches, and giving extra offerings to further God's work in their community and the world.

According to legend, King Arthur's magic sword, Excalibur, was only effective when it was used for the cause of good. Unfortunately for us, we are not guaranteed that kind of fail-safe system with all our resources. God has provided us with all that we need to be successful in our faith journey. We have our natural talents, physical resources, the fruits of the Spirit, the armor of God, and special gifts of the Spirit. But just like the heroes in today's fantasy stories, we must choose whether we will use these provisions for the cause of good or the cause of evil, or if we will allow them to just lie there and not be used at all.

Questions for Reflection

What gift from the fantasy stories would you most like to have and why?

What gifts and provisions has God given to you? What do you think might be your spiritual gift or gifts?

What talents do you have? How can you use these to serve God?

How have the fruits of the Spirit (Gal. 5:22–23) helped you in your journey?

What piece of the armor of God (Eph. 6:11–17) gives you the most comfort or aid in your journey?

What physical resources, such as a home, an automobile, a computer, or money, do you have? How can you use these to serve God?

How can these gifts and provisions help you fulfill your quest?

Traveling Companions: Friendship and Fellowship

When I arrived at Central Michigan University for my first year of college, I had no idea who my roommate would be. It turned out to be a guy named Jerry. Jerry and I had much in common. We both loved to play basketball, we both took our studies seriously, and we both attended church nearly every Sunday. But we had a number of dissimilarities as well. While I grew up in a small town in northern Michigan, Jerry grew up in the city of Detroit. I was a Protestant; Jerry was Roman Catholic. I tended to speak up for what I thought was right, no matter who I offended. Jerry encouraged me to be more sensitive to the feelings of others. I was inclined to see things in black and white; Jerry encouraged me to appreciate the shades of gray. Our differences led to tensions in our relationship, to be sure. But they also helped make our friendship one that was rich and rewarding. Jerry's friendship helped me grow as a person and as a Christian, and it helped me make it through the adventure that was my freshman year of college.

We are not called to journey alone. Besides the other gifts that God gives us, God gives us companions for our journey. According to the Book of Genesis, God said, "It is not good that the man should be alone" (Gen. 2:18), and created woman and man to be together. The *Epic of Gilgamesh,* one of the oldest writings known to the world, features the story of a king who learns the joy of finding a friend and companion. These ancient writings suggest that the life of a human being is incomplete without companions.

Friendship is one of the central themes of today's fantasy stories as well. Many readers and viewers see the Harry Potter stories, the original *Star Wars* trilogy, and *The Lord of the Rings* as, more than anything else, celebrations of friendship. These stories contain many beautiful illustrations of friendship that speak to us as powerfully as any sermon could.

The Harry Potter stories lift up friendship as one of the highest virtues in Harry's world. Several times the stories provide commentary on this point through the voices of reliable characters. In *Harry Potter and the Sorcerer's Stone,* honor student Hermione suggests that "friendship and bravery"[1] are even more important qualities than academic achievement. In *Harry Potter and the Prisoner of Azkaban,* Harry and Ron give Hermione the cold shoulder because, as they see it, Hermione has caused them to lose a prized broomstick and a pet rat. Hagrid, with his down-to-earth manner, is the voice of wisdom when he says, "I gotta tell yeh, I thought you two'd value yer friend more'n broomsticks or rats. Tha's all."[2] In Hagrid's words the reader hears a timely message for today's consumer culture—namely, that friendship is more valuable than possessions.

George Lucas has confessed that he knows that stories of friendship and loyalty might seem "corny" today, but he insists they are stories that need to be told.[3] The original *Star Wars* films (episodes 4 through 6) featured the troop of friends standing up for each other and bailing each other out of trouble time and time again. Some fans have noted that they miss some of this friendship and camaraderie in the more recent films (episodes 1 and 2).

In the same way, the very personal and intimate friendships among the hobbits anchor the epic scope of *The Lord of the Rings.* As Middle-earth-shaking events occur around them, it is Frodo, Sam, Merry, and Pippin's friendship and care for one another that draw the reader or viewer to care deeply about their journey and the results of their quest.

The Bible does not explore the theme of friendship in as much depth as we might expect.[4] There are, however, some glimpses of the value of friendship, what it means, and what it should be. We can reflect on several aspects of friendship by looking at the ways they are explored in the Bible and in today's fantasy stories.

Help along the Way: Friendship and Fellowship for the Journey

Hollywood movies have perpetuated the myth of the solitary hero, who by sheer force of will resolves a conflict on his or her own. These heroes may start out with a buddy or two, but they end up facing the problem alone. This is not a surprising motif for film. For one thing, this "one against the world" scenario makes for a dramatic story. Also, within the limits of a two-hour movie, it can be difficult to introduce and develop the number of characters that are usually needed to solve problems in the real world. In real life, however, we know that we need the support of other people to help us on our journeys.

The heroes of today's fantasy stories may stand alone at times, but overall the stories demonstrate that it takes a group of friends working together in order to accomplish a goal. As mentioned in the last chapter, in *Harry Potter and the Sorcerer's Stone,* it takes Hermione's intellect and logic, Ron's courage and chess playing skills, and Harry's flying skills and bravery to get past all the obstacles and make it to the Sorcerer's Stone. No one of them could have made it alone.

George Lucas's filmmaking style highlights this communal motif. The climaxes of many of the *Star Wars* films cut back and forth between several scenes as the battles are fought on many fronts. As a result, the viewer is presented with the image of many people working together and coordinating their efforts in order to achieve a victory. In *The Fellowship of the Ring,* Frodo Baggins acknowledges that he cannot complete his task alone; therefore a Fellowship is formed to help him on the way. In the course of the epic events that follow, the skills, knowledge, and experience of the entire Fellowship are needed to achieve success.

Besides the tactical advantage of working together as a group, having friends has personal benefits as well. Harry Potter would probably not be able to survive the stress of the dangers that confronted him if he were not able to share his burdens with his friends. For a time in *Harry Potter and the Goblet of Fire,* Harry and Ron are not talking to each other. Harry is clearly not at his best during this time, and the loss of Ron's friendship is almost too much for him to bear. In *The Two Towers* and *The Return of the King,*[5] it is clear that Frodo would not have made it very far without Sam. Sam lends some very practical support to Frodo, including finding food, cooking his meals, and literally giving him a shoulder on which to lean, but we understand that it is Sam's companionship, encouragement, and emotional support that are even more important to the success of the quest.

The Gospels imply this need for and value of friendship and fellowship as well. Although it may be true that in many ways Jesus walked his path alone, he did not set out on a solo journey. He gathered together disciples and chose twelve of them to be his closest companions. When he sent out seventy of his followers to heal and to teach about the Reign of God, he sent them out two by two (Luke 10:1). According to the Gospel of John, before his crucifixion Jesus prayed that, above all, his disciples have fellowship with one another:

> I ask not only on behalf of these, but also on behalf of those who will believe in me through their word, that they may all be one. As you, Father, are in me and I am in you, may they also be in us, so that the world may believe that you sent me. The glory that you have given me I have given them, so that they may be one, as we are one (John 17:20–22).

This prayer suggests that Jesus understood how important it would be for future disciples to have unity, and that this unity would be a sign to the world of the truth of the Gospel.

The Christian faith was founded as a communal religion. Jesus Christ founded a church—a community of believers that would join together for worship, learning, fellowship, and service. Christianity was never intended to be a faith that was lived out alone against the world. Instead, it is a faith that is lived out with companions to share the journey.

A Diverse Band of Travelers

Part of the inherent pleasure of many fantasy stories is in the way characters of diverse races, skills, and powers overcome their differences to join together and triumph over evil. In today's fantasy stories, characters must overcome their differences to join together in a common cause. In the process they discover that they are strong—not despite their diversity but because of it.

Diversity and inclusiveness are major themes of the Christian faith. It is true that, perhaps for cultural and practical reasons, Jesus' inner group of twelve disciples were all Jewish and male. They did, however, represent a diverse range of social classes, careers, and even religious sects. Women were prominent among his followers, were the people he healed and ministered to, and were notably present at the foot of the cross and the first to announce his resurrection. Jesus made women, Gentiles, and even Samaritans the heroes of his stories. Paul saw the wider-ranging, revolutionary implications of Jesus' Gospel, and proclaimed that in Christ, "There is no longer Jew or Greek, there is no longer slave or free, there is no longer male or female; for all of you are one in Christ Jesus" (Gal. 3:28). Sociologists and historians have suggested that the inclusive nature of the early church movement may be one of the reasons for its success. Because Christianity transcended race, class, and gender, it appealed to everyone and could use people's diverse strengths even within local communities of faith. In Christ the distinctions of race, culture, class, and gender are not barriers, but part of our strength.

These themes of racial, cultural, socioeconomic, and gender diversity exist in today's fantasy stories, and an exploration of each follows.

Racial and Cultural Diversity

Harry Potter, Ron Weasley, and Hermione Granger come from different types of families and different cultural backgrounds. Ron was born and raised in a wizarding family; Hermione was born and raised in a "muggle" (non-wizarding) family; Harry's parents were wizards (his mother with muggle heritage and his father with wizard heritage), but he was raised in the muggle world by his muggle aunt and uncle. In *Harry Potter and the Sorcerer's Stone,* these differences are of no consequence to the three friends and are not a barrier to their growing friendship. Diversity and tolerance become even more explicit themes in the later stories, when the friends run up against the bigotry and intolerance of others.

In the *Star Wars* films, *The Phantom Menace* and *Attack of the Clones,* viewers see beings of all races, shapes, sizes, and colors serving on the Jedi Council. This diversity is not explicitly addressed in the dialogue, but the use of wide-angle camera shots of the entire Council and cuts to close-ups of the various members of the Council make the point. The Council is a wise and respectable group of diverse individuals who work together and respect one another.

The individuals who make up the Fellowship of the Ring represent various races of Middle-earth. The Fellowship consists of four hobbits, a wizard, an elf, a dwarf, and two humans. Though they are a diverse group, they share the same goal, and it brings them together in "fellowship" (literally, "a sharing in common") to recognize one another's strengths. The Fellowship includes, for example, Legolas the elf and Gimli the dwarf. A racial and cultural feud has long divided the elves and dwarves. Legolas and Gimli each have justifiable pride in their own cultural heritage, and both harbor suspicions and distaste for the other's way of life. Legolas cannot stand the claustrophobic feel of the Mines of Moria or the way the natural rock had been cut and hewn to fit the vision of people. Gimli, of course, sees the mines as a glorious accomplishment of dwarven engineering and labor. And Gimli is at first frightened by and distrustful of the forests and tree houses of Lothlórien, while Legolas marvels at their beauty. Through the course of their journey together, however, they become the best of friends and learn to appreciate each other's culture. They promise each other that if they ever make it out of the war, Gimli the dwarf will visit the forest of Fangorn with Legolas, and Legolas the elf will visit the Glittering Caves of Aglarond with Gimli.

We might, however, wish for even more diversity on some fronts in the fantasy stories. Although these stories deal with cultural diversity at one level, the central human characters in the Harry Potter and *Star Wars* films are white. This could lead us to wonder if it is somehow safer to talk about race relations between pure bloods and mud bloods, Wookies and humans, or dwarves and elves than it is to deal with the very real race issues of our world today.

One of the biggest struggles in the early Church was of how to apply the unity of Christian faith to the diversity of cultural practices among new Christians (cf. Acts, chap. 15). Paul championed the view that one did not have to adopt certain cultural religious practices (in this case, Jewish practices such as keeping a kosher kitchen or the ritual of circumcision) to be considered a Christian in good standing. Many contemporary Christians may be unaware of the variety of ways that Christianity is practiced around the world. They may be surprised to discover that many of the things they believe to be essential parts of the Christian life are actually part of their own cultural practices. By adopting a global perspective, Christians can break down the barriers between different cultures and gain rich opportunities for fellowship across cultural boundaries.

Class Struggles

Today's fantasy stories suggest that class barriers should not prohibit friendship either. In the Harry Potter stories, the character of Draco Malfoy serves as the epitome of what a person should *not* be like. When Malfoy warns Harry not to hang around with the wrong sort of wizarding family—such as the working class Weasleys—the reader knows that Harry is right when he replies, "I think I can tell who the wrong sort are for myself, thanks."[6] Ron and Harry proceed to become the best of friends. Class struggles are addressed explicitly (if somewhat awkwardly) in *Harry Potter and the Goblet of Fire,* when Hermione founds the House-Elf Liberation Front. Although the humor may seem to trivialize the issue, Hermione and Dobby the house-elf's struggles do raise important points for reflection.

In *Return of the Jedi,* royalty and commoners are placed on an equal setting. We discover that Luke Skywalker, the boy from the rural moisture farm, and Leia, the famous princess, are really brother and sister. In addition, the ruffian Han Solo and the royal Princess find that they actually have much in common, and eventually they fall in love.

Overcoming class differences is also a central theme of *The Lord of the Rings.* It is said that during his service in World War I, J. R. R. Tolkien was moved by the way the soldiers in the war began to disregard the barriers of the British class structure of the day in order to form close friendships. Still, Tolkien's emphasis on the elite bloodlines of royalty can be disturbing, and today's readers may be uneasy with Sam's subservient attitude toward "Mister" Frodo. But the evolution of the relationship between Sam and Frodo, from servant and master to a friendship of two equals, undoubtedly made many of Tolkien's original readers just as uneasy, although for completely different reasons.

Just as Jesus' disciples had done before them, the early Church triumphed over cultural barriers and became a haven for poor and rich, slave and free alike. In the Epistle to Philemon, Paul urges Philemon to welcome back his runaway slave Onesimus, "no longer as a slave but more than a slave, a beloved brother" (Philem., v. 16). Several proverbs make the point that wealth or poverty should not be a barrier to true friendship (Prov. 19:4, 6–7).

Gender Barriers

Although women are not the lead characters in today's fantasy stories, the stories do include many positive examples of males and females becoming friends and working together for a common cause. In the Harry Potter stories, Hermione is a valued friend to Harry. Though other students suggest that there must be a romantic relationship between them, Hermione and Harry's friendship is proof that girls and boys can be platonic friends and excellent partners in adventure. At Hogwarts School of Witchcraft and Wizardry, girls and boys play together as members of the same Quidditch teams, and women serve together with men as respected members of the faculty. Still, the adult wizarding world sadly seems to reflect our world in that it appears that males are dominant in positions of authority in the Ministry of Magic.

The *Star Wars* films offer both positive and troubling images of women. The films offer strong female leaders in Leia Organa and Padmé Amidala, but even these strong female characters are at times exploited. In the opening of *The Return of Jedi,* Leia is reduced to a damsel in distress, exhibited in bondage and wearing a revealing slave outfit as a captive of Jabba the Hutt. And it is unfortunately predictable that in the arena battle in *Attack of the Clones,* it is only Padmé's form-fitting clothes, and not those of the men, that are ripped in the course of the fighting to reveal more of her body. Still, the films do show the value of women and men working together. These female characters are not relegated to specific gender roles, and they clearly take the initiative to enter into the fray side-by-side with the male characters.

In *The Lord of the Rings,* every central character—including all nine members of the Fellowship of the Ring—is male. But in some ways *The Lord of the Rings* offers the boldest feminist images of any of these three fantasy series. Lady Galadriel, and not her husband, Celeborn, is the voice of wisdom in Lothlórien. Arwen Evenstar, especially in the film version of *The Fellowship of the Ring,* is lifted up as a noble and powerful example of one who makes a conscious choice to exemplify sacrificial love. Éowyn, the Lady of the Shield-arm, refuses to be constrained by the traditional role of a woman. Readers can take delight at exclusionary language being revisited on the head of the perpetrator. When the Lord of the Nazgûl says, "No living man may hinder me!" Éowyn turns his exclusive language and thinking back on him, saying, "But no living man am I! You look upon a woman. Éowyn I am, Éomund's daughter. . . . Begone, if you be not deathless."[7]

It is true that, perhaps for practical as well as cultural reasons, Jesus' twelve traveling companions were male. But the Gospels make it clear that many female disciples followed Jesus faithfully and supported his ministry (Luke 8:1–3, 23:55–56, 24:10). Women also held prominent positions in the early Church, including Prisca, (sometimes called Priscilla) who, along with her husband, Aquila, was a courageous leader of the church in Ephesus (Acts 18:24–26, Rom. 16:3–5, 1 Cor. 16:19); Phoebe, a deacon (Paul does not use a separate word for "deaconess") of the church at Cenchreae (Rom. 16:1–2); and the daughters of Philip the evangelist, who had the gift of prophesy (Acts 21:9).

Diversity in Community and Individual Life

What value does diversity offer for our churches today? Many congregations have adopted a strategy of church growth that targets one specific demographic group. They design every program and worship event to meet the needs of a very specific group that shares the same cultural and socioeconomic background. Though this may be an effective marketing technique to baby boomers, there are several dangers to this approach. Most important, targeting just one group does not encourage the diversity inherent in the very concept of the Church and the Reign of God. But there are also practical considerations. First, younger generations are increasingly multicultural in their relationships and attitudes. They live in a world where the barriers of race, class, and gender have less and less meaning, and tend to stay away from social organizations such as churches that do not exemplify the diversity to which they are accustomed. Second, as many businesses and social organizations have learned, when people of all races, cultures, classes, ages, and genders sit side-by-side both in the pew and in key leadership roles, we are better able to understand and respond to the needs of our community and our world. When we are only around people who are like ourselves, we begin to get the idea that our way is the only way. Such thinking can lead to isolation—or even to attacking those whom we do not understand. Diversity enriches our congregations.

What about us as individuals? Do we have friends from different racial, social, or cultural backgrounds to enrich our lives while we are on our journey? These friendships may not come naturally or easily, but we will profit from the efforts we make to nurture new friendships that help us to see the world in new ways.

Surprising Friends

A common motif in many myths and legends as well as contemporary fiction is the revelation that an unassuming and unremarkable character is actually a great hero or royalty.

Harry Potter learns that the large and menacing looking Hagrid is a gentle soul. Behind Professor McGonagall's stern exterior we find a tender heart. And in reading the Harry Potter stories, we learn that we should never judge Defense Against the Dark Arts professors by their outward appearance!

In the *Star Wars* films, it would be easy to dismiss Han Solo as a rascal looking to make his next con. His character is presented as a simple, arrogant criminal who is only looking out for himself. But Han repeatedly surprises his friends by putting himself at risk. In *Star Wars: A New Hope,* he flies his ship to battle in the shadow of the Death Star to help Luke. In *The Empire Strikes Back,* he risks his life again by journeying into a frozen ice planet at night to try to rescue Luke. By the time viewers watch *Return of the Jedi,* they are not surprised to find that he has become General Solo and is leading a risky mission to deactivate the shield generator of the new Death Star.

One of the most well-known examples of this motif in twentieth-century literature is the story of Strider in *The Fellowship of the Ring.* At first Frodo and his friends do not trust this rough-looking ranger of the north. They have been warned to avoid him. But they quickly realize that he is much more than he appears to be, and they soon learn to love and trust him above all humans. Their trust is rewarded, as Strider is ultimately revealed to be Aragorn II, son of Arathorn, the last heir of Isildur and rightful king of Gondor and Arnor. As the poem about him suggests, "Not all that glitters is gold, not all who wander are lost."[8]

A variation on this motif is seen when characters are dismissed simply because they appear to be inconsequential, with little to contribute to the cause. In *Harry Potter and the Sorcerer's Stone,* the members of Gryffindor House discover that even their bumbling classmate Neville Longbottom has something to contribute to their pursuit of the house cup.

In *Return of the Jedi,* the small, furry Ewoks do not appear as though they would be of any help against the Imperial troops. Viewers take great pleasure in seeing these lowly creatures become key allies in securing the victory. The character of Yoda is a prime example of an individual who is underestimated because of appearances. In *The Empire Strikes Back,* when Luke Skywalker travels to the swamps of Dagobah to search for a great Jedi Master, he sees Yoda and immediately dismisses him as a small, silly-looking, silly-sounding, and totally inconsequential creature. Luke tells Yoda that he is looking for a great warrior, and dismisses Yoda by saying: "Now will you move along, little fella? We've got work to do." But much to his surprise, Luke soon learns that Yoda is the great warrior that he was sent to find.

In *The Lord of the Rings,* the hobbits Frodo, Sam, Pippin, and Merry are often underestimated. The fact that they are often quite literally overlooked actually works to their advantage, and helps them contribute to the task at hand.

Jesus was friendly toward those that others might have been eager to dismiss as crude or unworthy of attention. He was a friend to tax collectors and sinners (Matt. 9:11, Luke 7:34). He made the despised Samaritans the heroes of his stories, offering them as examples of true friendship. And he did not wait for people to change their ways before he was friendly to them. It is significant that Jesus went to the house of Zacchaeus, the tax collector, before Zacchaeus repented of his ways. Jesus recognized the worth in every person as a creature of God. To Jesus no one was of no consequence.

When Samuel is sent to David's house to anoint the next king, he at first assumes that David's older brother is the chosen one. But God tells Samuel, "Do not look on his appearance or on the height of his stature, because I have rejected him; for the LORD does not see as mortals see; they look on the outward appearance, but the LORD looks on the heart" (1 Sam. 16:7). We too may be surprised at the faithful friends we will find if we open our eyes to all people, including those who are different from us.

The Sign of True Friendship: Loyalty amid Adversity

True friendship is demonstrated through acts of loyalty in the midst of adversity. To their credit Harry Potter's friends stick with him, especially when times are tough. If anything, they are too loyal. Hermione perhaps compromises her own principles when she lies to the professors for Ron and Harry's sake. In *Return of the Jedi,* Luke Skywalker and the others put themselves at great risk to rescue their friends, and in so doing perhaps jeopardize the whole movement of the Rebellion. These risks are presented as virtuous behavior in these stories, which raises some questions for readers and viewers. Is it right to compromise one's own values for the sake of our friends? Should we jeopardize our great quest for the sake of friends? What should we do if a friendship or relationship is drawing us off the path of our faith journey?

In *The Lord of the Rings,* Frodo's friends demonstrate great loyalty. At the beginning of the quest, when they discover that Frodo must leave the Shire and head on a dangerous trip to Bree, Sam, Merry, and Pippin insist on sharing his danger. At Rivendell these friends again insist on continuing on the journey with their friend, even though it is not their duty or responsibility to do so. Finally, when the time comes for Frodo to leave for Mordor, Frodo desires to be a good friend, and he plans to go alone in order to keep the others out of harm's way. But Sam figures out Frodo's plan and runs after him. The scene in the film *The Lord of the Rings: The Fellowship of the Ring* is both humorous and moving. Frodo says, "No, Sam. I'm going to Mordor alone." Sam replies, "Of course you are, and I'm going with you." Frodo resists at first, but he is clearly happy when Sam insists on becoming his traveling companion. One of the most poignant themes in *The Lord of the Rings* is Samwise Gamgee's heroic friendship with Frodo. He stays beside Frodo even into the heart of Mordor. This loyal friendship, as it turns out, proves to be Frodo's salvation.

The Bible does not elaborate a great deal on the nature of true friendship, but one of the few criteria that it does lift up is that true friends remain loyal through adversity. David and Jonathan's friendship lasts through great difficulty and family conflict (1 Sam. 18—20; 2 Sam. 1:26). In the Book of Job, Job's friends stay beside him through his misfortunes, but it turns out that they stay around only to torment him. It soon becomes clear that they believe in their own theological dogma more than they do in their friend. According to several verses from the Book of Proverbs, the ability to stay loyal to someone through misfortune is a hallmark of friendship. Proverbs 17:17 reads, "A friend loves at all times, and kinsfolk are born to share adversity," and Proverbs 18:24 reads, "Some friends play at friendship but a true friend sticks closer than one's nearest kin."

Unfortunately, in the Gospels the twelve disciples are not great role models for loyalty in the face of adversity. Although they do follow Jesus through many hard times, they are unable to stay awake and keep Jesus company as he prays on the eve of his crucifixion. The Gospel of Mark tells us that they all left him at the end. Peter, the "rock," denied that he even knew Jesus. After the resurrection, however, the disciples become true friends of Jesus Christ. Church tradition tells us that they stayed loyal to him and his cause through great persecution and even death.

In the Gospel of John, Jesus offers the following words on friendship:

> No one has greater love than this, to lay down one's life for one's friends. You are my friends if you do what I command you. I do not call you servants any longer, because the servant does not know what the master is doing; but I have called you friends, because I have made known to you everything that I have heard from my Father (15:13-15).

To Jesus, then, true friendship has a cost. At times it obligates us to sacrifice our own needs and desires to help our friends.

Being a good friend can be hard work. It is not just a matter of having fun with people we enjoy being around. True friendship means sticking by people even when the going gets tough, such as when our friends are dealing with loss or disappointment. It means sticking with them when they are not at their best. While we are to be respectful and kind to all people, we are not obligated to become the best of friends to everyone who comes our way. We must choose our closest friends carefully and with our faith journey in mind.

Relationships are tough. At times it seems like it would be easier if our religion simply asked us to tune everyone else out and tune into God, or if it asked us to follow a set of rules and regulations so that we did not have to worry about others. But Jesus repeatedly confronted the Pharisees for caring more about the rules and regulations than about people. Jesus focused his teachings on how we must interact with and show love to others.

The examples from today's fantasy stories and the Scriptures can serve as an occasion to take inventory of our lives. If we do not have any friends, we may be challenged to work harder on nurturing friendships. These friendships will enrich our lives and help us live out Jesus' teachings to care for one another. We need other people to help us on our journey of faith. When choosing companions, we should not look just for people who look and act as we do. Our journey is enriched when we travel with diverse companions and when we do not discount the worth of potential friends with one glance. We are challenged to be loyal to our friends, even when the going gets tough. Christians were not meant to go it alone. We need traveling companions.

Questions for Reflection

Which character, or characters, from the fantasy stories would you most like to have as a traveling companion? Why? Which positive character from the fantasy stories would you least like to have as a traveling companion? Why?

Who are some of your best friends? Why are they your best friends? How did you become friends?

How have friends and companions helped you in your own faith journey? How have you helped them in theirs?

Have you ever had to show loyalty to a friend who was going through a hard time? Have you had friends demonstrate loyalty to you?

We naturally gravitate to people who are like us, but in so doing we often miss out on rich friendships. How can you nurture relationships with those who are different from you?

Have you ever had a surprising friend? Have you ever gotten the wrong impression of someone? Has anyone ever gotten the wrong impression of you? What lessons did you learn from the experience?

Staying on the Right Path (and Our Potential to Stray from It)

In *The Two Towers,* Samwise Gamgee wonders aloud whether Gollum sees himself as a hero or a villain.[1] It is a good question. In truth, we rarely recognize ourselves as villains, even when we are doing something that is evil. Even people of the deepest faith can be in danger of turning a blind eye to their own sinfulness. Many people do not believe that they are doing something wrong at the time they are doing it. Some who commit adultery say that they believed they were merely being true to love. Those who are selfish and greedy may feel at the time that they are merely learning to love themselves. Those in the church who viciously attack someone else's character or launch ruthless crusades against another group may feel that they are merely standing up for what is right. Those of us who are called to do good must come to grips with our own capacity for evil. Today's fantasy stories, along with the Bible, offer us the opportunity to reflect humbly on the unpleasant side that we all possess.

Our Capacity for Good and Evil

Like many of the characters in ancient myths, today's fantasy heroes are not cookie-cutter role models of good behavior. They demonstrate that they have within them the potential to do good and the potential to do evil.

In *Harry Potter and the Sorcerer's Stone,* every incoming student at Hogwarts is placed into one of the four school houses by a magical Sorting Hat that tells each student to which house she or he will belong. When it is his turn to wear the Sorting Hat, Harry Potter fervently hopes that it will not place him in Slytherin House. He knows that Slytherin House has a reputation for helping wizards achieve their questionable ambitions. Lord Voldemort himself was a member of Slytherin House, as were all other dark wizards that had ever come out of Hogwarts. The Sorting Hat's first impressions are disconcerting to Harry. The hat tells him that he could be great, and that Slytherin would help him on his way to greatness. But Harry pleads with the hat, urgently whispering *"Not Slytherin, not Slytherin."*[2] The Sorting Hat gives Harry his wish, and places him in Gryffindor House instead. But as he continues at Hogwarts, Harry becomes aware that he has many of the qualities necessary to become an evil overlord. As a matter of fact, in *Harry Potter and the Chamber of Secrets,* Harry discovers that he has a disturbing number of similarities with the evil Lord Voldemort himself. They look something alike, and both were orphaned and raised by muggles. They both speak Parseltongue (the language a few wizards use to talk to snakes), and both demonstrate great determination and resourcefulness. Harry and Voldemort also hold the only two wands that contain tail feathers from Fawkes the phoenix. Harry confesses to Professor Dumbledore that the only reason the Sorting Hat put him in Gryffindor House in the first place was that he had asked not to be put in Slytherin. Dumbledore responds by reassuring Harry that he is different from Voldemort precisely because he did not want to go into Slytherin. "It is our choices, Harry, that show what we truly are, far more than our abilities."[3] Harry learns that he is capable of doing good or evil, but that he must choose the path of good. By rejecting the ways of Slytherin, Harry is choosing to surround himself with a community of people who will help him walk the right path, and choosing to avoid those who would drag him down a darker path.

Luke Skywalker faces a similar revelation about himself. In *The Empire Strikes Back,* in the swamps of Dagobah, Yoda sends Luke into a tree cave that is strong with the dark side of the Force. When Luke asks what he will find there, Yoda responds, "Only what you take with you." In a powerful and frightening scene, Luke descends into the cave and faces Darth Vader. To Luke's horror, Vader's mask falls away, and Luke's own face is revealed underneath. He recognizes in himself the potential to become like Darth Vader. Luke understands that the evil that engulfs Vader could engulf him as well.

The character of Anakin Skywalker, later known as Darth Vader, demonstrates a wide range of potential for good and evil. In a scene that was deleted from *The Phantom Menace* but is available in the deleted-scenes section of the DVD, we see Anakin Skywalker saying farewell to the aged Jira. Jira asks for a hug, and says: "I'll miss you, Ani. You're the kindest boy in the galaxy." But there is no guarantee that Anakin will remain such a kind boy. As Qui-Gon Jinn says, "His fate is uncertain." Eventually we discover that this kind boy becomes one of the most evil people in the galaxy. Still, at the end of *Return of the Jedi,* after all that Darth Vader has done, Luke insists that there is still good in him.

In *The Fellowship of the Ring,* we find that even the lovable, innocent hobbit Bilbo Baggins is capable of evil. He takes to calling the Ring his "precious." In a horrifying scene at Rivendell, Frodo shows him the Ring, and Bilbo is momentarily transformed into a monster by his desire for it.

In *The Lord of the Rings,* Aragorn knows that humans are flawed and weak. They are not like the beautiful and immortal elves. But it is the imperfect, mortal races of humankind that become the focus of the story. The world has passed to them. Humankind, with all its flaws and all its potential to do good, is responsible for steering the future of Middle-earth.

In the Gospel of Luke, we read a parable that Jesus told "to some who trusted in themselves that they were righteous and regarded others with contempt" (Luke 18:9). The parable tells of a Pharisee and a tax collector who went to the temple to pray. The Pharisee offers a self-satisfied prayer, thanking God that "I am not like other people: thieves, rogues, adulterers, or even like this tax collector" (Luke 18:11). The tax collector, on the other hand, beats his breast and prays, "God, be merciful to me, a sinner!" (Luke 18:13). Jesus taught that it was the humble man who went home justified on that day. The parable illustrates how important it is for us to recognize our own sinfulness, and to recognize God's grace. Ironically, some

Christians today may read this parable and smugly pray, "Thank you, God, that I am not like that Pharisee."

Throughout the Bible we are reminded that we are not perfect and that we are capable of sin. The Bible is full of cautionary tales in which "heroes" such as Jacob and David commit horrendous and sinful acts. Paul writes, "For there is no distinction, since all have sinned and fall short of the glory of God" (Rom. 3:22–23), and that we must humbly acknowledge our need for God's grace, "For by grace you have been saved through faith, and this is not your own doing; it is the gift of God" (Eph. 2:8).

To stay on the right path, it seems we must come to a point where we truly recognize our own capacity for sin. This may come when we step back and take a realistic inventory of our lives. Perhaps we look back at behaviors that seemed fine at the time, but seem reprehensible to us now. With the perspective of time, we may realize just how cruel we were to a former boyfriend, girlfriend, or spouse when the relationship hit hard times. Or perhaps we are honest with ourselves, and remember just how many lies we have told to better our own position in life. In any case, recognizing our own capacity for good and evil will help us in several ways.

First of all, recognizing our capacity for good and evil will help us see that we are in God's good graces only because of God's mercy. This realization keeps us from being too smug and moves us to give thanks to God. Ironically, this attitude can be most difficult to attain for the most virtuous of Christians. Because they know that they are living a more virtuous life than most other people, they may fall into the trap of thinking that they are better than others. They may start to think of grace as something they have earned, rather than regarding it as God's unmerited favor to everyone.

Second, recognizing our capacity for sin gives us a realistic perspective on human nature. Though we look for the best in everyone, we do not naïvely expect the best from everyone. We cannot expect that everyone is always going to be honest with us, or that everyone else has our best interests at heart. We are called to "be wise as serpents and innocent as doves" (Matt. 10:16).

Third, if we acknowledge that we are all capable of sin, we will be better able to demonstrate the virtues of grace and forgiveness to others. The famous Bible commentator Matthew Henry was once robbed while traveling. In his diary that night, he wrote that he was thankful for four things: "Let me be thankful first, because I was never robbed before. Second, although they took my purse, they did not take my life. Third, though they took my all, it was not much. And, fourth, because it was I who was robbed, not I who robbed." As Christians we know that "there but for the grace of God go I."

Finally, recognizing that we are capable of sin helps us to stay on our toes spiritually. If we know that we ourselves, not just other people, are capable of evil, then we will be diligent in our spiritual lives. Our sinful nature can lead all of us to rationalize away our sins. We are tempted to frame our actions in ways that make us look noble. But when we recognize our own capacity for good and evil, we are called to reexamine our lives and our actions, and to avoid doing evil in the name of God.

Temptation and the Use of Power

In John Bunyan's classic allegory of the Christian life, *The Pilgrim's Progress,* the main character, Christian, has to face many obstacles and temptations that try to force him off the right path as he travels from the City of Destruction to the Celestial City. Christian runs into trouble when he tries to take shortcuts or the easy way around obstacles. In the same way, our faith journey is not only about reaching our destination; it is also about how we make the journey. To put it another way, it is not just whether we win or lose, but how we play the game. Part of the challenge of our spiritual life, then, is to stay true to our principles as we achieve our life's goals. We cannot take shortcuts by using immoral means to reach our ends.

Each of our heroes could have taken shortcuts to win individual battles, but in so doing, they might have lost the larger war. Harry Potter could learn spells that could help him in his battles against Voldemort. But in *Harry Potter and the Goblet of Fire,* we learn that while Professor Karkaroff has his students learn the Dark Arts at his Durmstrang School, Professor Dumbledore will only allow Hogwarts students to learn Defense Against the Dark Arts. In *Harry Potter and the Sorcerer's Stone,* Lord Voldemort promises to give Harry power and authority if only Harry will join him in his dark cause. Harry may be tempted to avoid the way of pain, but his unequivocal response to Voldemort is, "NEVER!"[4]

In the climactic scene of *The Empire Strikes Back,* Darth Vader tries to entice Luke to take the easy path with a variety of temptations. The first of these temptations is an appeal to the deep-seated desire for self-preservation. Vader says to Luke, "Don't make me destroy you." Next, he tempts Luke with flattery, saying: "You do not realize your importance. You have only begun to discover your power." He then tempts Luke with a noble goal, by telling him, "With our combined strength, we can end this destructive conflict and bring order to the galaxy." This is a worthy goal indeed, but the viewer can sense that Luke is making the right decision when he resists this temptation. Luke knows that he cannot achieve a good end by making a deal with a devil. Vader follows this by appealing to the seductive but less noble goal of power for its own sake. He tells Luke, "If you only knew the power of the dark side." Finally, Vader makes a very personal appeal. He tells Luke that he is Luke's father, and beckons him by saying: "Join me and together we can rule the galaxy as father and son. Come with me." Luke is offered the opportunity to join the parent he has never known. By the end of the scene, Vader has offered Luke a number of different reasons to choose a path that will take him away from pain and into power. It is clear that Luke *is* tempted; he is metaphorically and literally balancing on the edge of an abyss as he makes his decision.

Temptation and the use of power are recurring motifs in *The Lord of the Rings* as well. At the council of Elrond, those gathered realize that in the Ring they have a weapon of great power at their disposal. Boromir of Gondor at first argues that they should use this power to win their battles. But the others argue that this weapon of power is a weapon of evil, and therefore it must not be used but destroyed. The job of holding and guarding the Ring falls to Frodo Baggins. Along the way Frodo freely offers the Ring to Gandalf, Galadriel, and, in the film version, to Aragorn. Though they are all tempted, they each turn him down and recognize that in so doing they have passed a great test. Ironically, it is Frodo's willingness to give up the Ring that demonstrates that he is the one most qualified to bear the Ring and hold its power. In contrast, Saruman, Théoden, and Denethor want to hold on to power. They are corrupted by their desire to maintain whatever power they have to the point of compromising their virtue. In Middle-earth, it seems, real strength is demonstrated by one's ability to give up power or to share power with others.

According to the Gospels, Satan tempted Jesus in the desert by appealing to his physical needs with bread after he was fasting, to his personal sense of power by asking him to throw himself down from the pinnacle of the temple and have angels catch him, and to his political ambitions by offering Jesus all the nations of the world if he would just bow down and worship him (Matt. 4:1–11, Mark 1:12–13,

Luke 4:1–13). Jesus' response to these temptations is telling. He resists Satan's temptations by quoting Scripture back to him. Instead of the way of power, Jesus chooses the long, humble road to the cross.

The Gospel of Luke is quick to make connections between Jesus and Elijah and Elisha. But when, in a clear allusion to Elijah's defeat of the prophets of Baal (1 Kings 18), James and John asked Jesus to call down fire from heaven on the Samaritans who have rejected him, Jesus rebuked them (Luke 9:54–55). The Reign of God, it seems, was not to be implemented through acts of power and destruction, but by acts of mercy. Jesus taught a subversive way of using power. It is power that comes with traveling the extra mile and from loving our enemies. It is the power of mercy and love.

We may not believe that we have much power to use or abuse. But in fact we do have a great deal of power over those around us. On a personal level, we know only too well how to use our words to get in little jabs at a spouse's or a child's self-esteem. We can slip in little put-downs to hurt them and make them pay for some perceived past offense. We can use our power as a parent or a spouse to set up petty rules and to control others' behavior by making them do things our way. At work or at school, we can use our words to gossip or to drag someone else down in order to gain power or esteem for ourselves. On a corporate level, churches and church groups may be tempted to use power to achieve good ends in bad ways. What offends us in secular politics—behaviors such as backbiting, negative campaigning, twisting other people's words, or assassinating someone's character—often seeps into church politics as well. It is a sad truth that some of the most vicious examples of backbiting and character assassination happen in local church politics! To gain or maintain power and control over congregations, pastors and laypeople have given in to the temptation to use the most vicious of tactics. Christian political action organizations too have been known to use questionable means to grab power over others. But are we being true to our call when we try to accomplish our agenda at any cost? We can fall into the trap of using underhanded means to achieve our ends. Instead, we are called to do all that we do with integrity.

The Book of Romans suggests a subversive strategy for dealing with evil. To avoid becoming subsumed by the very evil we are resisting, it says, "Do not be overcome by evil, but overcome evil with good" (Rom. 12:21). Today's fantasy stories, along with the Gospels themselves, remind us that the end does not justify the means. In *The Empire Strikes Back,* Yoda tells Luke Skywalker, "The way of evil is the quick and easy path." We are called to resist the temptation to use whatever power we may have in a way that is destructive. As we work for change in our church, country, and world, we are called to do so in a way that is consistent with our principles. In this way we will stay on the right path as we travel on our faith journey.

Questions for Reflection

Several compelling scenes from the fantasy stories show heroic characters realizing that they are capable of evil. Which of these scenes made the greatest impression on you as you read the books or watched the films?

Has there been a time in your life when you recognized, not just intellectually but personally, that you were capable of sinning against others and against God?

What tempts you the most to stray off the path? What has kept you on the path?

Can you think of an example of when someone or some group of people used unjust means to try to achieve a noble end?

Have you ever had a position of authority or power that you were tempted to abuse? What helped you stay grounded and keep your perspective?

When are you tempted to use your power to make those around you feel badly? What keeps you from doing it?

Road Signs: Virtues in the Fantasy Lands

One of the functions of legends and myths is to pass on the virtues of a culture or belief system. The behavior of the heroes in these stories serves as an example of what the storyteller presumes to be morally excellent behavior. As George Lucas put it, it is through myths that we pass on the meat and potatoes of a society from one generation to the next.[1] Unlike philosophical essays that may advocate various formulas for moral reasoning, these stories have the power to show virtuous behaviors that readers or hearers can relate directly to their lives.

The Harry Potter stories, the *Star Wars* films, and *The Lord of the Rings* offer many good examples of how a virtuous person should act. By reflecting on which behaviors are presented in a positive light and which behaviors are presented in a negative light, we begin to get a sense of what each story lifts up as virtues. As with most works of fiction, these stories also contain some behaviors that we might find questionable. These are discussed in the final section of this book, "Dangers along the Path."

This chapter begins with a discussion of selected virtues that are featured in the Harry Potter stories, the *Star Wars* films, and *The Lord of the Rings* respectively. Next, it explores key virtues that are shared by all three series. Finally, it discusses the difficulties we may face when we try to use the Bible as a book of virtues or even as a book that features faithful role models.

Virtue at Hogwarts

Tolerance

Diversity and inclusiveness are themes in all three of today's popular fantasy series. The theme of tolerance, however, is especially repeated and highlighted in the Harry Potter stories. Words of prejudice and elitism are put into the mouths of Draco Malfoy, Professor Snape, and Delores Umbridge, characters that are established as negative examples in the stories. In *Harry Potter and the Chamber of Secrets,* Malfoy calls Hermione a "mud blood," an offensive slur against wizards who are not born of wizarding parents. In *Harry Potter and the Prisoner of Azkaban,* Snape despises and mistrusts Animagi, wizards who can transfigure into animals. In *Harry Potter and the Goblet of Fire,* we learn that Malfoy and many others in the wizarding world mistrust giants, assuming that anyone with giant blood must be evil and dangerous. In contrast, Albus Dumbledore, who functions as the reliable voice of wisdom in the stories, has no problem including all types of people in the Hogwarts community. This tolerant attitude is not always popular, but Dumbledore, along with Harry, Ron, and Hermione, boldly stands against acts of prejudice and exclusion anyway.

The series also features a personal story of the power of both tolerance and intolerance. Harry's family and his classmates in the muggle school that he attends as a child both fear and despise him because he is different from them. Harry is a wizard trapped in a non-wizarding world. Harry's childhood serves as a metaphor for the way that many children experience life; they feel that they are different and that somehow they do not belong. One of the most moving aspects of the first book is the way that Harry is received at Hogwarts. For the first time in his life, he is not seen as a freak. He is accepted for who he is.

The Gospel of Luke especially highlights Jesus' tolerance and acceptance of others. Jesus was criticized for socializing with tax collectors, prostitutes, and other sinners. He healed lepers, who were rejected by their communities, and then told them to see a priest so that they could get a clean bill of health and be accepted back into society (Luke 5:12–14). He encouraged his disciples to follow the example of a Samaritan who rose above religious, racial, and cultural prejudice to help a man in need (Luke 10:29–37). He told his followers to live by the virtue of love for all people, and to avoid judging and condemning others (Luke 6:27–38). And while he did not condone their immoral behavior, Jesus did not condemn those who sinned (John 8:1–11).

Today's pilgrims find themselves in a diverse, multicultural world. More than ever we live side-by-side with people who look and live differently than we do. Groups like the Nazis, the Ku Klux Klan, and al-Qaeda share in common the opinion that everyone around them should look, act, think, and believe as they do. In their view, no one else should be tolerated. In contrast, Christianity is a faith that challenges us to accept others even as we hold firm to our own beliefs. In order to succeed on our faith journey, we need to learn about our neighbors, and learn to love them even when they are different from us. Tolerance is a virtue for our faith journey.

Virtues in the *Star Wars* Universe

Discipline and Self-control

Many of today's action and adventure films feature heroes who get angry, shoot, and then stop to think about it. Their lack of discipline and self-control is often presented as a kind of virtue. In contrast, the *Star Wars* films lift up the virtue of being in control of our anger and our actions. In *The Empire Strikes Back,* Yoda teaches Luke Skywalker that the Force is to be used only for knowledge and defense and not for aggression. In the climactic scene of *Return of the Jedi,* the evil Emperor tries to persuade Luke to forget his discipline and act on anger. He taunts Luke, saying: "The hate is swelling in you now. Take up your Jedi weapon. Use it. . . . Give in to your anger." This dilemma is presented as Luke's ultimate test in the trilogy. Will he be able to control his anger or will he give in to the dark side?

In the Sermon on the Mount, Jesus taught his followers to respond not in anger but in love (Matt. 5:21–26, 5:38–48). According to Matthew's and Luke's Gospels, one of Jesus' followers drew a sword and cut off the ear of one of the slaves of the high priest who had come to arrest Jesus. Jesus' response is instructive. In Matthew's Gospel Jesus responds by warning his disciples that "all who take the sword will perish by the sword" (26:52). In Luke's Gospel he shouts, "No more of this!" and then heals the man's ear (Luke 22:50–51). In both cases his actions teach the way of self-control. The Apostle Paul listed self-control among the fruits of the Spirit (Gal. 5:22–23), and compared himself in his spiritual journey to an athlete who "exercises self-control in all things" (1 Cor. 9:25).

Today's pilgrims find themselves in a culture that is becoming increasingly familiar with terms like "road rage," "air rage," and even "spectator rage." Lack of impulse control is cited as a cause for the increase in such social ills as street violence and addiction. How can we avoid reacting to stressful situations with violent or self-destructive behavior? We can nurture the virtue of self-control in several ways in our own lives. We can explore some of the many stress management and anger management books, Web sites, or classes to help us reduce stress so that we are not always living on the edge of a blowup. We can find time away from life's distractions for meditation and prayer to nurture our relationship with God and create a sense of serenity. The words *disciple* and *discipline* come from the same root, so we should not be surprised to find that, if we are to be faithful disciples, we must learn to practice discipline and self-control.

Faith

In the *Star Wars* films, faith in things unseen is considered a virtue. In *Star Wars: A New Hope,* viewers hear Han Solo dismiss what he calls "hokey religions and ancient weapons." But this is immediately followed by a scene in which Ben trains Luke to sense the Force. Viewers witness Luke, with his eyes covered, deflecting ray blasts with his ancient lightsaber just by sensing them. Han says that Luke is just lucky, but viewers know better. In the enemy camp, Admiral Motti criticizes Darth Vader's "sad devotion to that ancient religion." Vader responds by saying, "I find your lack of faith disturbing," and makes Motti start to choke with the slightest twitch of his hand. In the *Star Wars* galaxy, faith gives a person self-knowledge, inner strength, meaning, and purpose. Faith also gives people the power to accomplish the mission at hand.

In a key scene in *The Empire Strikes Back,* Luke Skywalker's X-wing fighter sinks into the swamps of Dagobah. Luke moans,

"We'll never get it out." Yoda responds: "So certain are you. Always with you what cannot be done." Yoda then instructs Luke to raise his X-wing fighter out of the swamp using the Force. Luke tries, but fails to do it. When Yoda tells him to keep trying, Luke complains, "You want the impossible." In a dramatic scene heightened by swelling music, Yoda himself proceeds to raise the ship. Luke watches in amazement, and says, "I don't . . . I don't believe it." Yoda replies, "That is why you fail."

In the opening scenes of *The Phantom Menace,* Qui-Gon Jinn and Obi-Wan Kenobi are attacked by a seemingly overpowering number of battle droids and destroyer droids on a Federation battleship. But they do not panic. They do not give up. Throughout the stories of the *Star Wars* universe, Jedi Knights calmly face what appear to be overwhelming odds. But they have faith that an unseen Force in the universe will help them overcome their hardships.

The Book of Hebrews offers a well-known definition of faith:

> Now faith is the assurance of things hoped for, the conviction of things not seen. Indeed, by faith our ancestors received approval. By faith we understand that the worlds were prepared by the word of God, so that what is seen was made from things that are not visible (11:1–3).

The word *faith,* however, does not carry the punch today that it did when the biblical authors used it. Today faith is often used to refer to a mere belief or mental assent that something is true. As it is used in the Bible, faith means something more.

In the New Testament, to have faith in something or someone is to trust in it and rely on it. If you have faith in something, you show clear commitment and devotion to it, even though the object of faith cannot be confirmed by empirical observation. This way of understanding faith helps us understand why the Book of James suggests that faith without works (that is, good deeds) is worthless (2:14–20). The kind of faith that comes with trust and true commitment will naturally lead us to good deeds.

The faith discussed in the Bible is also not simply a faith in one's self or an optimistic perspective. For Christians, of course, the object of faith is God, who is revealed in Jesus Christ. It is this trust in God put into action that carries the true power of faith. The scene in *The Empire Strikes Back* in which Yoda raises the ship from the swamp is reminiscent of Jesus' teaching of the power of faith in the Gospel of

Matthew. The disciples were unable to cure a boy possessed by a demon, but Jesus does the impossible by curing him. Jesus told his disciples, "[I]f you have faith the size of a mustard seed you will say to this mountain, 'Move from here to there,' and it will move; and nothing will be impossible for you" (Matt. 17:21).

Faith is also more than a one-time assent to certain doctrines or creeds. It is a process by which we grow more committed to God and to God's call to us. The Book of Hebrews speaks of running the race set before us, "looking to Jesus as the pioneer and perfecter of our faith" (12:2). As we place our trust in the ultimate goodness of God, our trust is confirmed and our faith can grow as we become ever more confident in our walk with God (2 Cor. 10:15–16). It is this faith that grants us power for the journey.

Virtues in Middle-earth

Knowing Our Ancient Stories and Songs

In *The Lord of the Rings,* virtuous people, including strong warriors, wise wizards, and even humble gardeners, demonstrate knowledge and respect for the ancient stories and songs of their people. The time they spend learning about their spiritual and literary heritage is not depicted as an odd pastime, but rather as a sign of their strength of character. Strider's knowledge of the songs of old is presented to the reader as an early indication that there is far more to this ranger of the north than meets the eye. Although reading and learning songs were not common practices in Sam Gamgee's family, his knowledge of the poems and songs he heard from Bilbo lets others know that he has a depth of character that may not be immediately apparent. Throughout their quest, characters in *The Lord of the Rings* take time to remember stories of old and relate them to their own time and place. These stories and songs are not just idle trivia or dusty old history; they are living stories. Noble characters in Middle-earth understand the significance of these stories for their own time, and they recognize themselves as part of an ongoing story.

To some people it may seem strange that Christians spend so much time and effort learning ancient stories and poems from bygone ages. But Christians understand the writings of the Bible and stories from Church history to be more than dusty old history. They are part of our spiritual heritage. They are living stories and through them we can see ourselves as a continuing part of God's ongoing story in the world. The time we spend learning about the Bible and our spiritual heritage is not time ill spent; it is a noble undertaking. By seeing our life stories in the context of God's ongoing story, we can understand our faith journey more clearly.

Hospitality

In *The Hobbit,* twelve dwarves descend on Bilbo Baggins's home for tea, and exhibit what is for hobbits quite rude behavior by proceeding to eat and drink him out of hobbit hole and home. Readers may wonder why on earth Bilbo puts up with it. The answer is that Bilbo was simply exemplifying a virtue that any good hobbit would practice: hospitality.

The theme of hospitality is clearly established and reinforced by repetition in the book *The Fellowship of the Ring.* Frodo and his companions are the recipients of gracious hospitality again and again as they travel on their journey. Farmer Maggot and his wife not only offer Frodo and his friends a warm meal, but mushrooms to go. Maggot also risks his own life to see the travelers further down the road. When they are in danger in the Old Forest, Tom Bombadil and Goldberry, daughter of the River, prepare for them a great meal and soft beds, and then send them off with a song and a promise of safety. Barliman Butterbur, the innkeeper of the Prancing Pony, offers them rooms for a fee, it is true, but he offers them very nice rooms. When he realizes that he has put them at a disadvantage, he goes to great trouble to help them, and even purchases the pony Bill for them to take on their way. In the House of Elrond at Rivendell, Frodo and his friends rest in the home of the elves and are once again given supplies to take on their way. They are welcomed in the woods of Lothlórien, and the Lady Galadriel herself gives each member of the Fellowship a special gift to help them on their journey.

In each of these cases, the travelers are first tested by their hosts, but then are accepted with great warmth and generosity. They are even given gifts to take on their way. It would be difficult to overstate how important these acts of hospitality are to our heroes. The respite and care that is given to them is what empowers them to continue on their difficult journey.

The hospitality demonstrated by those in Middle-earth parallels the hospitality that was practiced in the ancient Near East. Welcoming strangers into one's home was a common courtesy (cf. Gen. 18:1–8). Once a stranger was deemed safe, he was fed, given lodging, and sent on his way with a blessing. According to the Gospels, Jesus did not take too kindly to those who refused to show hospitality to him or his followers. According to the Gospel of Mark, Jesus expected that his disciples would be offered hospitality when on a mission (Mark 6:10). And in Luke 7:36–50, we read that Jesus publicly reproved Simon the Pharisee for his lack of hospitality. In Jesus' famous words concerning the separation of sheep and goats, the criterion he uses to separate the faithful from the unfaithful is whether or not they have shown hospitality to the hungry, the thirsty, the naked, the stranger, and the prisoner. Jesus said that when we give or withhold hospitality to "the least of these who are members of my family" (Matt. 25:40), we are giving or withholding hospitality to the Son of Humanity himself (Matt. 25:31–45). Jesus is teaching his followers that he is incarnate in those who need our care and hospitality.

The early Church also expected its members to give and receive hospitality (Acts 17:7, 21:17, 28:7; Rom. 12:13; 1 Pet. 4:9). "Do not neglect to show hospitality to strangers," the Letter to the Hebrews goes so far as to say, "for by doing that some have entertained angels without knowing it" (13:1).

Hospitality seems to be a fading art today. In a fear-filled world, we want to protect our privacy and avoid inviting others into our homes or into our lives. We also tend to take the attitude that what's ours is ours, and others should not expect us to provide them with anything. But most of us can remember times in our lives when others welcomed us and cared for us in big and small ways. It would be hard to overestimate the importance of acts of hospitality, which may sustain us for the rest of our faith journey.

These memories of being welcomed and cared for challenge us to offer hospitality to others. This may mean inviting a college student to a weekend away from campus, providing a busy couple with a warm home-cooked meal, or something more. Many Christians have found that hospitality is their primary gift and calling in life. They welcome those who are new in town, may become foster parents, or may adopt children who are in need. Churches live out the call to hospitality through their ministries to refugees, starting and supporting shelters for those who are homeless, supplying travel expenses and lodging for those who are far from home, or welcoming strangers into their faith communities. While we are busy with our own faith journeys, we should remember that others on the journey sometimes need a safe haven from life's storms.

Shared Virtues

Because the Harry Potter stories, the *Star Wars* films, and *The Lord of the Rings* all explore spiritual themes, it is not surprising that several key virtues are demonstrated by the heroes of all three series. Some of these virtues have already been discussed in earlier chapters, such as the virtues of friendship, loyalty, and love of learning. Other key virtues, such as perseverance, hope, and sacrifice, will be explored in later chapters. What follows is a list of more key virtues from these stories that are also shared with the Christian story.

Humility and Respect

Chapter 2 of this book suggested that we must not think too highly of ourselves, even as we stay aware of how special we are in the eyes of God. The discussion of humility in that chapter focused on how we need to keep a proper view of ourselves. The virtues of humility and respect as they are discussed in this chapter, though, relate more directly to how we view and treat others.

Harry Potter demonstrated humility and respect in a small way in *Harry Potter and the Prisoner of Azkaban* when he bowed respectfully to Buckbeak the hippogriff. By bowing and deferring to the hippogriff, a dangerous creature with the head and wings of a giant eagle and the body of a horse, Harry gained its trust. This small gesture of courtesy kept Harry safe from a potential enemy, and more important, gained him a friend who would help him in the future.

In the same way, in *The Phantom Menace,* Queen Amidala gets on her knees and humbly acknowledges the authority of Boss Nass, ruler of Jar Jar Binks's Gungan people. Boss Nass is impressed by this gesture. It indicates to him that Queen Amidala does not think that she is any better than the Gungans, and consequently he agrees to help her. Amidala's small gesture of humility wins her the allies she needs for the battle to come.

In *The Return of the King,* Merry and Pippin bring their hobbit virtues of humility and respect to high places. Their thoughtful and respectful words to King Théoden and Denethor II, the steward of Gondor, secure these valuable allies for the cause of the Fellowship.

The New Testament lifts up the virtue of humility as well. Jesus cautioned his followers against presuming to take on places of honor for themselves, and instead encouraged them to show respect to others. He warned them that those who try to exalt themselves will be humbled, while those who humble themselves will be exalted (Luke 14:7–11). Paul also encouraged this virtue, especially within the church. Apparently he observed people using the church as a place to promote their own importance. So he encouraged members to treat one another with humility and respect, suggesting that this was one of the keys to unity (Rom. 12:3, Eph. 4:2).

Another important practice is that of honoring one another. It is easy to see the lack of this virtue when observing the sibling rivalries of children, many of whom struggle to get more attention and honor from their parents than their brothers and sisters. But many adults continue this childish behavior. They resent the success of others, and spend much more time and energy lifting themselves up than they do looking for opportunities to build up others. Today we need to recognize that the honor and respect that others gain—especially the honor and respect that we ourselves give—does not diminish us but lifts us up as well. If we want to be competitive, Paul suggests a healthy competition: "Love one another with mutual affection; outdo one another in showing honor" (Rom. 12:10). Instead of being preoccupied with our own status in our workplace, family, or church, we can better spend our time by consciously looking for opportunities to compliment, lift up, and affirm others. By demonstrating humility and showing respect to others, we not only help others move forward on their journey, we gather companions and friends for our journey as well.

Connection to Nature

It may seem surprising that today's blockbuster movies—filled with state-of-the-art digital special effects—carry what might be seen as an old-fashioned message. To varying degrees all these stories speak to our need to connect with the natural world.

The wizarding world of Harry Potter has little need for what Mr. Weasley calls "eckeltricity" (electricity) or machinery that has been invented by the muggle world. And while Dudley Dursley spends his time playing Mega-Mutation: Part Three on his PlayStation, Harry prefers to spend his time with his owl, Hedwig, or outside playing Quidditch. At school Harry and his classmates learn about magical plants and animals in Herbology class and in their Care of Magical Creatures lessons. Through these classes they learn to appreciate nature as it exists in their magical world.

Perhaps surprisingly, this back-to-nature theme is even more pronounced in the *Star Wars* films. At the end of *Star Wars: A New Hope,*

Luke Skywalker abandons the use of technology by turning off his targeting device and using only the Force. Darth Vader himself serves as a cautionary example: by the end of his life, his very body is made up mostly of machinery. He has allowed technology and machinery to eclipse his humanity. Both of the *Star Wars* trilogies feature tales in which more natural, organic communities, the Ewoks and the Gungans, defeat armies that are more technologically advanced. *Return of the Jedi* draws a sharp visual contrast between the cold, sterile look of the Empire's technology and the warm, bright earth tones of the Ewok village. In the commentary on the DVD edition of *The Phantom Menace,* George Lucas acknowledges that some might find it ironic that while he loves to use the latest technology, he uses it to tell stories that warn against losing ourselves to technology. Lucas makes it clear that he is not opposed to the use of technology in general; rather he is concerned with the way some technologies can be used to disconnect us from our humanity and the natural world.

Connection to nature is a recurring theme throughout *The Lord of the Rings.* Hobbits live in hobbit holes that are literally built into the earth. Elves integrate their dwellings and their lives into the forests that surround them. The film *The Lord of the Rings: The Fellowship of the Ring* explores this connection to nature in a visually memorable way. An awe-inspiring tracking shot begins with the image of Gandalf on top of a tower speaking respectfully to a moth, then moves to the contrasting image of orcs tearing apart forests and burning them to manufacture weapons of war. In *The Two Towers,* Treebeard, the ancient treelike creature who watches over the trees of Fangorn Forest, voices his worry that humans do not have enough respect and concern for the forests. This theme is given a more personal dimension at the end of the trilogy. The four hobbits, Frodo, Sam, Merry, and Pippin, return to Hobbiton only to find that industrialization has spoiled their home. The trees are torn down, the groundis dug up, and smoke billows out of smoke stacks. But it is no coincidence that Tolkien has made his "common person," Samwise Gamgee, a gardener. In the end it is up to Sam to use a special gift from the Lady Galadriel to restore the land.

In biblical times people did not have the same environmental concerns that we have today. People were not clear-cutting forests, disposing of large amounts of manufactured chemicals, or burning fossil fuels on the scale that we do today. They did not have to be encouraged to get out and observe God's creatures and creation, because they did not have the option of avoiding it by living their lives in hermetically sealed buildings and vehicles. Therefore we would not expect environmental concerns to be addressed in the Bible in the same way that we address them today. Still, the Bible contains important principles that serve as a foundation for our concern and care for creation.

According to the Bible, God created the world and called it very good (Gen. 1:31). The Psalms proclaim that the earth, the sea, and the dry land belong to the Lord and proclaim God's glory (24:1–2, 95:5, 148:9–10). It is of no small significance, then, that God has called humankind to be stewards of this creation (Ps. 8:4–6, Gen. 1:28–30).

We have many practical ways to incorporate our concern for creation into our daily lives. We can start by recycling; buying recycled materials or items with minimal packaging; reusing household items such as cups, thereby cutting down on the amount of trash we produce; and limiting our use of fossil fuels by trying to carpool or use public transportation when possible. We can become active advocates for the environment as it relates to public policy issues.

Many people find that one of the best ways for us to nurture concern for the environment is to spend time in nature. By spending time with all of God's creation, we learn to appreciate it and grow more committed to preserving it. Many have found an important fringe benefit to this enterprise: when they increase their connection to creation, they find that they are nurturing their connection to the Creator as well.

Courage to Act

In many ancient myths and legends, heroes confront monsters and enemies with extraordinary courage. They make bold decisions to face enemies and confront evil, apparently without giving it a second thought. Part of the appeal of today's fantasy stories is that while they depict actions that are no less courageous, their heroes seem to be more like us. They have weaknesses and fears and doubts. But they also have courage and strength of character. By the time our heroes perform their heroic deeds, their actions do not seem extraordinary. Instead, their deeds seem to be natural manifestations of their character. Yes, they are being courageous, but because we have come to know the characters and what they stand for, their actions do not surprise us. These heroes are not part of some superhuman pantheon of characters who know no fear. They are simply people of virtue, committed to carrying out their calling despite their fears.

In the Harry Potter stories, it is significant that Harry, Ron, and Hermione belong to Gryffindor House, which values courage over other virtues. We know that they are just three schoolchildren, but on several occasions they courageously walk into the valley of the shadow of death. Although Luke Skywalker first appears in *Return of the Jedi* as a brave and bold Jedi Knight, we soon learn that he still makes mistakes and that he knows fear. Yet he does not balk at confronting danger. In *The Lord of the Rings,* Aragorn must overcome his self-doubt and fear of failure to be the leader that Middle-earth needs him to be. We are impressed with Frodo and Sam's courage to go on because we are aware that they are afraid—and yet they continue on anyway.

Paul writes that Christians are to "keep alert, stand firm in [their] faith, be courageous, be strong" (1 Cor. 16:13). Christians are told that they can have courage because they know that Christ has the ultimate victory over the forces that stand in their way (John 16:33, Acts 23:11, 2 Cor. 5:6–7).

Although Christians believe that Jesus was divine, they also believe that he was fully human. On a wholly human level, it is hard not to be impressed with Jesus' courage to go through with his crucifixion. The Gospel of Mark tells of his fear and despair at Gethsemane. He was "deeply grieved" (Mark 14:34), but was determined to follow God's path for him. Jesus provides a model of courage.

Courage is not simply a naïve lack of fear. It is the virtue of standing up for our convictions and doing what must be done even when we understand the dangers and difficulties it will bring. The courage that is exemplified in the fantasy stories and urged in the Bible is the courage to put our convictions into action. Sometimes courage can drive us to do great things in the face of great danger. People who have taken part in civil rights movements across the globe have known that they were putting their lives on the line, but they have stood firm and lived out their calling. Sometimes courage is put into action by making a major change in our personal life. It may take a great deal of courage to leave a job or a relationship that is secure, but that we know is not healthy for our relationship with God. We may need courage to stand up to others at work or school in smaller ways by refusing to laugh at jokes that demean others, feed into gossip, or go along with unethical plans or policies that would compromise our faith. Whether we are making bold leaps or taking small steps, we need to have courage to live out our faith.

Mercy and Forgiveness

Forgiving others is one of the hardest things we are called on to do, especially when someone has betrayed our trust. At a time when many films play to our very human desire to get vengeance on those who have wronged us, the Harry Potter stories, the *Star Wars* films, and *The Lord of the Rings* trilogy prominently feature the virtues of mercy and forgiveness.

In *Harry Potter and the Prisoner of Azkaban,* Harry has the chance to execute the man who betrayed his father and mother to Voldemort and caused their death. Harry shows the man mercy, despite his feelings of hatred toward him. At the end of the story, Dumbledore explains to Harry that this seemingly worthless act of mercy may prove to be beneficial to Harry in the long run.

In *The Empire Strikes Back,* Lando Calrissian betrays his old friend Han Solo by handing Han, Leia, and Luke over to Darth Vader. By trying to understand Lando and the plight he was in, Han and the others are able to forgive him. In so doing they gain a valuable ally. Luke Skywalker must have had a host of grievances against his father. Not only did Vader fail to raise him and his sister, he betrayed the entire Jedi Order and the cause of freedom. The central story of the original *Star Wars* trilogy (episodes 4 through 6) culminates in Luke embracing a merciful attitude toward his father and seeing the good in him.

In *The Lord of the Rings,* Boromir, a member of the Fellowship, betrays Frodo. Later Frodo meets Faramir, who is Boromir's brother—a fact that is unknown to Frodo. But when Frodo speaks to Faramir about Boromir, his words are kind, forgiving, and sincere. This forgiving attitude not only gets Frodo out of a tight spot but also wins him a friend and an ally.

In the film version of *The Lord of the Rings: The Fellowship of the Ring,* it is in the Mines of Moria that Frodo, who knows that the creature Gollum is the cause of their troubles, says to Gandalf, "It's a pity Bilbo didn't kill him when he had the chance." Gandalf replies: "Pity? It was pity that stayed Bilbo's hand. Many that live deserve death. Some that die deserve life. Can you give it to them, Frodo? Do not be too eager to deal out death and judgment."[2]

Frodo and Sam eventually have the opportunity to follow Bilbo's example. They each spare Gollum's life, even after he tries to betray them to death. In the end these shocking, unreasonable, and heroic acts of mercy turn out to be their salvation.

Forgiveness is, of course, one of the cornerstone principles of the Christian faith. The Gospel itself is the story of how God forgives humankind despite their sins against God and God's ways. In the Lord's Prayer, Jesus taught his disciples to pray, "And forgive us our debts, as we also have forgiven our debtors" (Matt. 6:12). Immediately after teaching the prayer, Jesus explained, "For if you forgive others their trespasses, your heavenly father will also forgive you; but if you do not forgive others, neither will your Father forgive your trespasses" (Matt. 6:14–15). Jesus seems to suggest that we need to forgive others in order to truly understand and receive forgiveness ourselves.

Jesus had the chance to put his words into action in his own life. He was betrayed several times—not only by Judas Iscariot. While Jesus was being crucified, his disciples abandoned him. Peter even denied that he ever knew Jesus. On a larger scale, the whole world, including those who crucified him, was rejecting Jesus. According to the Gospel of Luke, while Jesus hung dying on the cross, he looked at those who were crucifying him, and prayed, "Father, forgive them, for they know not what they are doing" (Luke 23:34). Although these people—like many who wrong us today—may not have recognized the full implication of their actions, they still had to know that what they were doing was not kind and merciful. They knew that they were killing Jesus, and yet Jesus still forgave them. After Jesus' resurrection, he apparently held no bitterness toward his unfaithful disciples. He told them to be at peace and, according to the Gospel of John, made a special effort to affirm Peter for his future ministry (John 21:15–19).

Forgiveness, especially of those whom we feel have betrayed us, may be one of the most difficult virtues for us to practice. Forgiveness is the virtue that moves us morally and spiritually beyond the limits of right and wrong, me versus you, or my religion versus your religion. Yet forgiveness stands as one of the central principles of the Christian faith.

Why is forgiveness so important for our faith journey? Perhaps one reason is that if we let grudges and bitterness fester, they can eat at our souls and prevent us from making any progress in our faith journeys. Many of us have felt betrayed at one time or another by coworkers, fellow students, family members, spouses, former spouses, or others. As modeled in today's fantasy stories, forgiving someone does not mean that we should accept that person into our life as though he or she were our best friend. As a matter of fact, in cases where we have been hurt or abused, it is best that we avoid that abusive relationship. Harry Potter, for example, did not become best chums with the man who betrayed his parents to death. But he did not let his anger at the man consume him or control him. He did not harm him when he had the chance. He continued to live by his own virtues of mercy and forgiveness.

So what does it mean to forgive someone? Does it mean we must pretend that we have not been wronged by another person or that we cannot feel anger toward them? No. Acknowledging our anger, talking through it, and working through it may be important steps in moving toward forgiveness. Forgiving someone who has betrayed us does not mean that we must deny our emotions, but it may mean that in our heart we no longer wish them ill, and that we do not spend our time and energy worrying about them or speaking ill of them to others. It means that we move on in our journey and no longer let their act of betrayal hold power over our life. This is hard to do. Forgiveness is an extraordinarily heroic act. But if we cannot forgive, we may find ourselves stalled on our journey.

The Bible As a Book of Virtues?

Many children's Bibles and videos try to turn the Scriptures into a book of virtues or into the stories of Bible heroes who serve as perfect role models. But the characters of the Bible are not often portrayed as models of virtuous behavior in the Bible itself. As a matter of fact, Bible heroes model many vices. Abraham lies about having a wife and puts her in danger (Gen. 12:10–20); Jacob schemes and cheats his brother out of his birthright (Gen. 27); Moses kills a man (Exod. 2:11–15); David commits adultery and has his mistress's husband killed (2 Sam. 11); the disciples lie and abandon Jesus at the end of his life (Mark 14:50, 66–72); and the apostles of the early Church quarreled amongst themselves (Acts 16:36–40, Gal. 2). It is difficult to find any character besides Jesus who consistently demonstrates positive virtues. On the other hand, many Christian novels and storybooks that are written today are full of picture-perfect Christian role models who come off as unrealistic and uninteresting. In contrast, the Bible often draws us into realistic, complex lives, and leaves it up to us to work out prayerfully how it might apply to our lives.

As we read through the Bible, we discover that much of it is more concerned with our relationship with God than it is with lessons in morality. Many Christians would be quick to point toward the Ten Commandments and the Sermon on the Mount as familiar examples of great moral teachings. But even these passages warrant a closer look. The first five commandments, at least, seem to be more concerned with our relationship with God than with doing right and wrong, and it would be a mistake to reduce it all to a list of moral values. Much of the Sermon on the Mount is focused on understanding God and the Realm of God, rather than moral teaching. This is not to say that virtuous behavior is unimportant. Surely one of the missions of the Christian Church is to teach the way of Jesus. But there is a danger of being like the Pharisees and reducing religion to a set of do's and don'ts.

Narratives with real and living characters demonstrate a variety of behaviors, good and bad. At their best, these narratives can inspire us to virtue. But it is still up to each reader and viewer to work out and apply what they read to their own life. We cannot expect to read the Harry Potter stories or *The Lord of the Rings* and find that every likable character always does the right thing. In fact, it is dangerous to look at any one character as a perfect role model. Still, some of the actions of these fictional characters can serve to inspire us and remind us of the virtues of our faith.

Questions for Reflection:

Which of the virtues discussed in this chapter do you think you do a pretty good job of practicing in your life?

Which virtue do you struggle with the most?

Can you name someone whose life often exemplifies one of these virtues? How is that virtue demonstrated in her or his life?

Can you think of a virtue that was not mentioned in this chapter, but that you think is an important one?

Who do you need to forgive today? Is he or she still a part of your life? What do you need to say to him or her?

Do you need to receive forgiveness from someone else? What steps can you make toward asking for forgiveness?

Creatures of the Dark: Vices in the Fantasy Lands

From the earliest of times, people have told stories of monstrous creatures that lurk in the dark. They have often used these creatures to represent the dark and ugly parts of human nature. In ancient legends and myths, as well as in today's fantasy stories, these evil creatures take many forms. This chapter does not provide a comprehensive bestiary for these stories, but instead pauses to look at some of their monsters and discuss what they say about what is evil, how we overcome it, and how we can avoid becoming monsters ourselves.

Creatures from Harry Potter

In keeping with the series' theme of tolerance for those who look or act differently, the monstrous creatures in Harry Potter's world are often not evil at all, but just misunderstood. Rubeus Hagrid's love for dangerous creatures, such as dragons, hippogriffs (griffins), the three-headed Fluffy, and even the great spider Aragog, is presented as a virtue—or at least an endearing eccentricity. With a few notable exceptions, it is the humans who are the real monsters in Harry Potter's world.

Dwelling on Guilt and Regret

In *Harry Potter and the Prisoner of Azkaban,* Harry is faced with creatures known as dementors, who feed on the pain, guilt, and regret of others. Harry's friend Hagrid spent a short time being imprisoned by dementors in the wizarding prison of Azkaban. Hagrid tells Harry that the dementors made him keep going over the most horrible events of his life again and again, and says that being released from the prison was like being "born again."[1]

According to the story, it appears that dementors can be resisted in two ways. One way is to create a patronus, a magical white light that drives away the dementors. Harry is told that he can create a patronus by thinking happy thoughts. Harry, however, finds that it takes more than happy thoughts to drive away the sorrow and pain of his past. It takes the much deeper and more profound feeling of joy. For Christians this joy comes from knowing that we belong to a loving God who cares about us. Jesus encouraged his disciples to abide in God and in God's love, "so that my joy may be in you, and that your joy may be complete" (John 15:11). As he prepares for his own death, Jesus fervently prays for his disciples, "so that they may have my joy made complete in themselves" (John 17:13). To know God is to know joy.

We learn that a second way people can resist dementors is by having confidence that they do not carry with them a burden of guilt. In the book, a notable prisoner of Azkaban is able to survive long exposure to the dementors because he knows that he is innocent. The dementors could not bring him into despair when they tried to make him dwell on his guilt. In the same way, because Christ has provided the sacrifice for sins that brings forgiveness, Christians are told that they can draw near to God with full assurance of faith and without a guilty conscience (Heb. 10:22). For Christians, of course, one of the great joys of their faith is knowing that although they may be guilty of many sins, they are forgiven, and they are no longer prisoners of their guilt.

Christianity is a religion whose very gospel is that of forgiveness and release from guilt. It is sadly ironic, then, that many Christians live as though they have a dementor at their side every day. They live in dementor-like prisons of their own making. They do not forgive themselves, and therefore will not allow themselves to accept God's forgiveness. As a result they are not able to move forward in their faith journeys. Others are stuck in the saddest moments of their lives, living in the past and going over the saddest or most regrettable moments of life again and again. They are stalled in their faith journeys and cannot become the joyful Christians God would have them be. People who find themselves in these situations may need traveling companions to help them move forward. By meeting with pastors and counselors, many Christians find that they can open themselves up to the joy and forgiveness of the Christian faith. Not only are they helping themselves when they do this, they are empowered to help others as well. They become living examples of the redeeming power of God's grace.

Unfortunately, some well-meaning Christians can turn into dementors themselves! They have twisted the Gospel in such a way that they see it as their job to remind others repeatedly—their children, their spouse, members of their congregation, or even strangers—of their past sins and shortcomings. These dementors feel that it is their duty to make sure that others pay for their sins and do not get off the hook. Little comments here or a harsh remark there makes others feel that they are being judged by the worst moments of their life. As a result, many of the people around them never truly experience God's love and forgiveness. We must take a close look at ourselves to make sure that we never turn into dementors. Instead of using matters of faith as a cage, we can offer the gospel as a key out of prisons of shame and guilt.

To be all that God would have us be, we must truly accept the gospel of joy and forgiveness. At the same time, we must be messengers of that gospel to others. We are called to be instruments of God's mercy, not instruments of judgment. If we fail to do this, and instead take on a crusade of making others dwell in their sin and guilt, we just might become monsters ourselves.

Deeds Done in Secret

In *Harry Potter and the Goblet of Fire,* the Death Eaters are a secret society of those who support the evil Lord Voldemort and share his disdain for muggles and for wizards who are not from pure-blood wizarding families. When they go out in public, they go in the dark and wear masks and robes to hide their identity from others. They may be mere humans under these disguises, but they are some of the most frightening creatures of all.

Secret societies such as the Ku Klux Klan and other terrorist groups know that they cannot stand up to the light of day and therefore hide in secret meeting places or under hoods. Although they may convince themselves that they are being noble by standing up for their beliefs, subconsciously a part of them must know better. Instead of pursuing their goals openly, they try to achieve their ends by fear and intimidation. They plot and plan in secret.

According to the Gospel of John: "For all who do evil hate the light and do not come to the light, so that their deeds may not be exposed. But those who do what is true come to the light, so that it may be clearly seen that their deeds have been done in God" (3: 20–21). If our actions and causes are true, we should not fear to act openly.

On a personal level, some of us might convince ourselves that our own questionable actions are justified and not really hurting anyone. We may take work supplies home in a purse or smuggle extra cafeteria food out in a backpack, even though it is against the cafeteria's policy. We feel that these actions are somehow justified in the grand scheme of things. One way to test ourselves is to see if we feel comfortable doing these actions openly and in the light. If the people in charge really do not mind, then we have nothing to fear from being open about it. On the other hand, if we feel morally obligated to oppose an unjust rule or law, then we should be willing to follow the examples of Gandhi and Martin Luther King Jr. These civil rights leaders practiced a form of protest known as civil disobedience. Civil disobedience calls us to demonstrate the courage of our convictions by opposing unjust policies and practices openly, exposing them to the light. In this way we can effect a change. If we believe in our cause strongly enough, we will be willing to pay the price.

Creatures from *Star Wars*

Acting on Anger and Aggression

The *Star Wars* films feature a plethora of monstrous and imaginative creatures, such as the rancor from Jabba the Hutt's dungeon in *Return of the Jedi,* and the reek, nexu, and acklay from the arena scene in *The Attack of the Clones.* These creatures are not well developed in the story, but if they have any personality trait in common, it is that they appear to share a proclivity toward aggression and violence. They tend to strike out first and think later. This often works to our heroes' advantage, as they are able to get the creatures to rush ahead and become stuck quite literally between a rock and a hard place.

Many of the lead characters in today's action and adventure movies seem to share these monstrous traits, and yet they are featured as the heroes rather than as monsters! When they get angry, they lash out with fists, guns, and explosives. Films feature this sort of violent action for several reasons. First of all, it is a popular fantasy to imagine that we can make our problems go away just by lashing out when we get angry. Young children often get mad and hit when they do not get their way. But as adults we know that anger and violence rarely, if ever, solve our problems. Another reason for violent resolutions in films is that over the course of a two-hour movie, the hero does not have enough time to ponder nonviolent solutions to his or her problems. It takes time and patience to think through alternative solutions; it is quicker and easier just to blow up the enemy. A final reason for this sort of violent resolution in films is that it is, quite frankly, visually more interesting than watching people stop and think through their problems and arrive at a solution. Although aggression and violence are usually rewarded in action and adventure films, we know that when we act out of impulse and anger in the real world, it usually only serves to make matters worse. We get ourselves caught between a rock and a hard place, just like the creatures in the *Star Wars* films.

Jesus told his disciples to avoid anger and violence by turning the other cheek (Matt. 5:39) and seeking the way of peace. This does not mean that people should never feel angry (see Mark 3:5), but that we are not to act on our anger with aggressive acts against others. As the Letter to the Ephesians puts it, "Be angry but do not sin" (4:26). The Book of Proverbs offers us centuries-old advice on how to avoid becoming creatures of anger. It tells us, "A soft answer turns away wrath, but a harsh word stirs up anger" (15:1), and, "Those who are hot-tempered stir up strife, but those who are slow to anger calm contention" (15:18). These words could come straight out of a modern-day conflict resolution seminar. When we act out of anger, we cause all sorts of problems. With harsh words or vengeful actions, we can take a bad situation and make it worse. Conversely, when we respond to anger with calm and understanding, we can often take a bad situation and make it better.

Another way to avoid becoming creatures of anger ourselves is to avoid getting drawn into the angry and bitter mindset of those around us. This may mean that we need to avoid getting too close to friends, colleagues, or family members who constantly speak out of anger and bitterness. They can have a negative effect on our morale and our outlook on life.

The images of the aggressive creatures in the *Star Wars* films getting stuck and defeated can serve as a cautionary metaphor for our own angry behavior. When we are tempted to speak out or strike out in anger, we might imagine that we are going to look heroic and powerful. But it is much more likely that when we act in anger, we will end up looking as silly as those *Star Wars* creatures that get themselves stuck in traps of their own making and then thrash around and complain. We would be wise to avoid becoming creatures of anger and aggression ourselves.

Conforming to the Masses

Villains and monsters are often depicted as either total loners or part of the mindless masses. *The Phantom Menace* introduced battle droids as an obedient but ineffective army for the forces of evil. They are ultimately defeated because they cannot think for themselves. The battle is won simply by destroying one central mind that controls them all. In a similar way, *The Attack of the Clones* introduced the production of a clone army that would not have much individuality and could be easily controlled.

Human history is filled with stories of atrocities that occurred simply because large groups of people passively went along with the evil and misguided will of a few. Large groups of people may be persuaded to conform through words that appeal to the worst parts of human nature. Contributing to these horrors is simple peer pressure. When "group think" takes over, individuals no longer think for themselves. They ignore their own conscience for the sake of avoiding disagreements with those around them.

Christianity values community, of course, but it is a religion that also values individual initiative and conscience. Christians are not called simply to go along with the prevailing ideology of the day or to defend the status quo. As the Apostle Paul wrote, "Do not be conformed to this world, but be transformed by the renewing of your minds, so that you may discern what is the will of God—what is good and acceptable and perfect" (Rom. 12:2).

Our world needs both unity *and* diversity of thought. People of faith are called to be prophetic voices against unjust situations that most people seem to accept as normal. Even atrocities such as slavery have been taken for granted as a way of life in many societies, though acceptance does not mean that evil and unjust practices have ever been right. Many people of faith have refused to become like droids or clones and have had the courage to stand up and speak out against injustice.

Christian communities need to guard against becoming congregations of droids or clones as well. Some congregations want their members to conform completely to a detailed set of doctrines, share the same taste in music, and even take on certain clothing styles and mannerisms. These congregations run the risk of becoming like cults. They would gain wisdom and strength by opening themselves up to include and accept people with a variety of perspectives and approaches to their faith.

Creatures from *The Lord of the Rings*

Greed and Materialism

In the tradition of European dragons, the dragon Smaug lies alone in his lair in the Lonely Mountain, hoarding his treasure and guarding it jealously. Although he is presented as a mighty and marvelous creature of great power, he strikes readers of *The Hobbit* as a sad creature. Even with all his riches and treasure, Smaug is never truly satisfied or fulfilled. He is a picture of greed and materialism. He spends his life being paranoid, hoarding and protecting his treasure, but never truly enjoying it. Of course we should not be too harsh in our judgment of Smaug. After he is gone, we find that elves, men, dwarves, goblins, and a wolf-horde fight the bloody Battle of Five Armies over the same treasure.

Gollum, one of the most pathetic characters in twentieth-century literature, does not have a huge hoard of treasure. Instead, he comes into possession of just one treasure, the One Ring, and it consumes him. He is literally twisted and deformed by his desire for it. Like Smaug, Gollum no longer possesses his treasure; it possesses him.

According to the Gospel of Matthew, Jesus warned his followers to keep their priorities straight:

> Do not store up for yourselves treasures on earth, where moth and rust consume and where thieves break in and steal; but store up for yourselves treasures in heaven, where neither moth nor rust consumes and where thieves do not break in and steal. For where your treasure is, there your heart will be also (6:19–21).

In our materialistic culture, we are constantly bombarded with messages telling us what we need to own and consume. In this environment we have a real danger of subconsciously being convinced that our task in life is to be consumers. We are convinced that we need to "get it now" and "collect all five!" We are in danger of letting our possessions possess us.

The vice of materialism can be exacerbated by our enjoyment of these fantasy stories themselves. A huge amount of merchandise is created based on these series. Some of the products provide healthy ways to engage the stories in new ways and on a number of levels. All these series have inspired collectable card games that can engage fans of all ages in creative and educational interactions with others. There are excellent BBC radio dramas of both *The Lord of the Rings* and *Star Wars*, and the Harry Potter books are brilliantly performed on tape by actor Jim Dale. Hearing these stories on tape is like experiencing them again for the first time.

It may be a helpful exercise to take an inventory of our Harry Potter, *Star Wars*, and *The Lord of the Rings* collections. We may be surprised at how much money and time we have spent collecting action figures, deluxe editions, and other memorabilia. Though there is nothing wrong with having a hobby or collection, we may want to ask ourselves if we truly need all these things. Might some of that time and money be better spent on doing and supporting God's work?

Weaving Webs of Deceit

Shelob the Great is the last of the Great Spiders of Middle-earth. She created a complex web in which to ensnare those who passed her way. All living things were her food. She was not only evil in and of herself, but her evil also served to protect the evil of Sauron.

Christians know that people are fallen and capable of evil acts. We must be on our guard so that we are not ensnared in the traps and schemes of others. The epistles describe the devil as a wily schemer who is trying to ensnare us (2 Cor. 2:11, Eph. 6:11). Christians often look for the good in everyone, but they are warned against being naïve and believing that everyone is good and trustworthy. Jesus warns his disciples in the Gospel of Matthew that we are to "be wise as serpents and innocent as doves" (10:16).

We also need to guard against becoming schemers ourselves. Some of us may find ourselves setting up traps for other people with our words. We might ask a question or bring up a topic with a plan of using the other person's words against them in the future. Through gossip and negativity, we can spin a web and slowly suck the life out of those around us for our own purposes and to feed our own egos. If we find ourselves scheming to dishonor or bring down others, we know that we have gotten off track on our faith journey.

The Love of Destruction

Orcs are the creatures who make up the armies of evil in *The Lord of the Rings.* They take pleasure only in destruction and pain. They tear down the forests and destroy others for pure enjoyment. Not only do they destroy their enemies, they often destroy each other.

In the Gospel of John, Jesus draws a contrast between himself and those who destroy. He says: "The thief comes only to steal and kill and destroy. I came that they may have life and have it abundantly" (10:10). Paul tells the Thessalonians to "encourage one another and build up each other, as indeed you are doing" (1 Thess. 5:11).

Our calling is to build up others and build up the cause of righteousness. We are to be constructive and not destructive. We should be concerned if we find that most of our energies are going into tearing down others and other viewpoints, or that we spend more time arguing against something we see as negative rather than supporting something positive. This is not to say that we should let go of our convictions, but rather that we should work for change in a positive way rather than a negative one. In this way we can be creative creatures of the great Creator. In this way we will stand firm in our convictions but avoid destroying others. In this way we will avoid becoming orcs, seeking to destroy others in the name of our faith.

The Evil One: Not Just Some Body

In today's fantasy stories, the forces of evil are not just humans who are restricted to a human body. In the Harry Potter stories, Lord Voldemort survives the destruction of his body several times over. The evil, it seems, outlasts the person. In the *Star Wars* universe, the Sith are people who are adept at drawing on the Dark Side of the Force, but they are not the Dark Side of the Force itself. In *The Lord of the Rings,* Sauron the Dark Lord is killed in ancient times, yet he continues to exist as a disembodied spirit of evil until he can grab hold of power again. Throughout *The Lord of the Rings,* Sauron remains "off screen" during the action, highlighting his nature as a force of evil rather than an individual person. Although these evil ones may not have physical bodies, they exist in these stories as long as people support them and nurture their evil power.

In the New Testament, Satan represents the forces of evil that Jesus battles to establish the Reign of God on Earth (Mark 3:23–26). As with the evil ones in today's fantasy stories, Satan represents a personification of evil in the Bible. And just as is the case in the fantasy stories, defeating the power of evil is not as simple as destroying one person. The Gospels are not just the story of Jesus and his twelve knights, who simply hunt down Satan, defeat him, and declare the battle won. The battle against evil is not that direct. When seventy of Jesus' disciples return from their mission, they tell Jesus that demons had submitted to them. It is then that Jesus says, "I watched Satan fall from heaven like a flash of lightening" (Luke 10:17–18). It is the faithful demonstration of God's healing power, and not a direct assault on an individual, that is the initial indication that Satan is a defeated foe (John 12:31). According to the Letter to the Ephesians, no mere physical battle can defeat the evil one: "For our struggle is not against enemies of blood and flesh, but against the rulers, against the authorities, against the cosmic powers of this present darkness, against the spiritual forces of evil in heavenly places" (6:12).

We cannot picture these spiritual battles as easily as we can picture the physical battles that are often depicted in fantasy stories. It is not surprising, then, that the Book of Revelation uses vivid fantasy imagery to depict the ultimate battle between good and evil. Christ is represented by a rider on a white horse (19:11), and Satan is represented as a dragon (12:7–9). Despite evil's great power, it is ultimately defeated by the power of God (20:1–10).

What lessons are learned from looking at evil as a force or power rather than a physical entity? For one thing, it cautions us against demonizing individuals as the embodiment of all that is evil. At times we can let grudges grow until we picture another person as the great Satan himself. In *Return of the Jedi,* Luke Skywalker was able to look at Darth Vader and recognize some good in him. Vader gives evidence that this is true by repeatedly finding reasons to spare Luke's life. Christians believe that evil exists in the world, but they also know that by the power of God, all humans are redeemable. It is the power of evil that needs to be defeated, not other people.

Second, though it is true that evil is not embodied in any one person, it is also true that evil finds its greatest expression through the lives of human beings and human institutions. In other words, it is not simply an evil cloud that sweeps over us and destroys us. We see and experience evil through other people, and through the systems of business and government that people set up. It is our responsibility as people, then, to resist evil and prevent it from finding expression through us.

Third, if we envision evil as a force that is not limited to a single human body, our method of resisting it will change accordingly. We find that sacrifice and redemption are more effective than aggressive assault, which will be discussed in the chapters that follow.

Finally, although many of the villains in fantasy stories take on traditional visual forms, the nature of the evil that is described in the Bible and in these stories cautions us against expecting evil to look only like Darth Maul. As a matter of fact, Darth Maul's devilish look of red skin and horns is not taken from a biblical image of the devil at all, but from later myths and legends. More often in Harry Potter, *Star Wars*, and *The Lord of the Rings,* we find that the evil one and his allies, such as Tom Riddle, Senator Palpatine, and Saruman, deceptively appear in the form of friends with persuasive tongues.

The monstrous creatures of fantasy stories can serve as cautionary images of what we must avoid in order to be successful on our faith journey. Unfortunately, at times they can also serve as mirrors that help us see the dark and ugly sides of ourselves.

Questions for Reflection

As you read or watched the stories, which creature from the fantasy stories was the most frightening to you?

Which vice do you struggle with most when it is present in others?

Which vice do you struggle with most in yourself?

What is your own understanding of Satan, or the evil one? How do you resist evil in your life?

How are you working to overcome evil and injustice in the world?

Rough Roads Ahead: Hope and Hard Times

When I was serving as a pastor in Connecticut, a teenager in our church who had been going through a rough time committed his life to Jesus Christ and the Christian faith. He was baptized and became a member of the church. It seemed as though his life turned around overnight. He was doing better in his studies at school, becoming more popular, dating a nice girl, and even getting along better with his mom at home. He was taken aback, then, about eight months later, when he came on hard times again. He was struggling in some of his classes at school, he did not get a job that he wanted, it looked as though he and his girlfriend would break up, and his plans to go to college were not falling together the way he had hoped they would. We went to a park to talk about it all, and I was just about to try to encourage him when he turned to me with a smile and said: "You know, Russ, I guess being a Christian doesn't mean that you never have hard times. It just means you know that things can get better. Now I know that things can get better."

The Promise of a Rough Road, or "I've Got a Bad Feeling about This"

Sometimes people are accused of living in a fantasy world if they imagine that everything is wonderful and that they do not have any problems. Hogwarts, the *Star Wars* universe, and Middle-earth certainly do not fit this image of fantasy worlds. The heroes of today's fantasy stories do not find themselves in carefree wonderlands, but instead in worlds filled with danger and sorrow.

In *Harry Potter and the Sorcerer's Stone,* Harry is happy to be escaping the unhappy world of the Dursleys, but he quickly learns that he is entering a world filled with dangerous creatures and dark wizards. He soon finds himself facing dangers that range from being mocked by his fellow students to being attacked by a mountain troll.

The *Star Wars* universe contains its own troubles and dangers. In *The Empire Strikes Back,* Luke Skywalker sees the daunting task ahead of him but musters up the bravado to say, "I'm not afraid." Yoda's chilling response to Luke is: "You will be. You will be." The characters repeatedly find themselves in dangerous spots. A running joke in the *Star Wars* films is that in each film the characters face such dangerous situations that at least once someone is prompted to repeat the line, "I've got a bad feeling about this."

In *The Fellowship of the Ring,* one gets the impression that both Gandalf and Strider wish they could shield Frodo, Sam, Merry, and Pippin from Middle-earth's dangers. But they know that they must warn the four innocent hobbits of the dangers they will face in the wider world. In the film *The Lord of the Rings: The Fellowship of the Ring,* Strider asks Frodo, "Are you afraid?" When Frodo admits that he is, Strider's reply is, "Not nearly enough." The path ahead of the Fellowship is a difficult one, full of struggles and dangers.

In the same way, the Bible tells us that the way of faith does not guarantee smooth sailing on the journey. As a matter of fact, we are promised rough roads ahead. The Gospel of Matthew tells the story of a scribe who says to Jesus, "Teacher, I will follow you wherever you go" (8:19). Jesus' immediate response is to say to him, "Foxes have holes, and birds of the air have nests; but the Son of Man has nowhere to lay his head" (8:19). At first Jesus' response may strike readers as a non sequitur, an irrelevant response to the scribe's statement. But Jesus was making an important point. The scribe was enthusiastic and eager to follow Jesus. But Jesus wanted to warn him immediately of the consequences of his choice. Following Jesus would be hard work. Jesus explained that he and his followers did not even have regular lodging for their journey.

Again and again Jesus warns those who want to follow him that they will face difficult times. Jesus tells his disciples, "See, I am sending you out like sheep into the midst of wolves" (Matt. 10:16). He tells stories of people giving up everything they own to take part in the Reign of God (Luke 15). When crowds followed Jesus to hear his teaching, he warned them that they would have to carry the cross in order to be his disciples (Matt. 10:38, Luke 14:27). Although those who heard Jesus may not have understood the full implications of his imagery of the cross, they would have understood that Jesus was warning them that they would face a difficult life if they were to follow him. The Gospels proceed to tell us of Jesus' own journey toward personal sacrifice. Jesus was not a masochist. If he could have found an easier way, he would have been only too happy to take it. But, as Jesus prayed to God at Gethsemane, he was willing to follow the path set before him, whatever the cost might be (Mark 14:36).

The Christian faith, then, does not promise us an easy road if we become faithful Christians. On the contrary, it almost guarantees that we will have rough times if we live our lives faithfully. The epistles of James and 1 Peter tell Christians that rather than being surprised by trials and persecution, they should expect persecution if they stand up for God. Instead of looking at these trials as a reason to question their faith, the writers of 1 Peter and James invite Christians to use them as an opportunity to grow in their faith, trusting that God will see them through (James 1:2, 1 Pet. 4:12). We are not promised an easy and smooth path on the Christian journey. We must expect trials along the way.

Perseverance for the Journey

In the *Star Wars* films, the droid R2-D2 provides a helpful image of persistence. R2-D2 repeatedly saves the day by stubbornly and deliberately doing what must be done. In *Star Wars: A New Hope,* even though Luke's family purchased R2-D2, the small droid insists that he belongs to Obi-Wan Kenobi and sets out to find him. While other characters may hesitate because of doubt or fear, R2-D2 simply sees what needs to be done and does it. Sometimes we need to be like R2-D2, just doggedly committed to our mission and to doing what it takes to get the job done, whether we feel like it or not.

In *The Fellowship of the Ring,* most of the Fellowship's time is spent not in exciting battles or glamorous settings but simply hiking over rough terrain for long distances. During these parts of their journey, their work must have seemed mundane and tiresome, but by diligently putting one foot in front of the other, the Fellowship was getting the Ring to the place where it needed to be. The burden of this task grew heavier and heavier for Frodo and Sam as they approached Mordor. In the end Frodo was so determined to reach the Cracks of Doom that he insisted on going forward even if it meant he had to crawl on his hands and knees to make it there.

The writer of the Book of Hebrews in the Bible may have been alluding to the Olympic marathon runners of old when challenging believers to "run with perseverance the race that is set before us" (12:1). We are empowered to run the race of our faith by looking at the examples of faith that have come before us (Heb. 11). The early Church was commended for the way they endured in their work for God under the most difficult situations (Rev. 2:2, 2:19).

Sometimes we have wonderful and exciting mountaintop experiences in our spiritual lives. We might have great spiritual insights or have the opportunity to do ministries in which we can clearly see what we are accomplishing, and perhaps even receive public acclaim because of our work. But at other times we need to trudge uphill one step at a time to get to that mountaintop. On any given day, we may not *feel* the joy or excitement of living a life of faith. It may not seem glamorous to pray or to donate our time to a charitable organization doing work that will not be seen by many. We may not feel like being polite to others, or saying, "I love you" to a child or spouse who needs to hear those words from us. It may not seem heroic to put our money in the offering plate each week. At times like these we need to persevere. Sometimes our faith journey is simply a matter of putting one foot in front of the other and doing what is right, simply because we know that it is right and needs to be done.

Hope Calls Us Forward through the Darkness

One of the most powerful gifts that God gives us to navigate over rough roads is the gift of hope. Samwise Gamgee serves as an excellent example of a hopeful spirit. Throughout *The Two Towers* and *The*

Return of the King, Frodo and Sam stumble on—despite the odds—because of the glimmer of hope for success in their task. Sam is a realist; he knows that they might not make it. But despite that, Samwise serves as a bearer of hope. At the darkest of times, when Frodo is tempted to give in to negativity and despair, Samwise heroically holds out hope that they might succeed and encourages Frodo to keep going.

In the New Testament, hope is one of the primary motivations for living a faithful life. According to the Gospels, Jesus told his disciples that they could endure trials and tribulations because they have the hope that someday, in some way, it will be revealed that God is ultimately in control and will reward them for their faithfulness (e.g., Luke 6:20–38). The concept of hope was a vital part of the Apostle Paul's message. In his First Letter to the Corinthians, Paul lists hope, along with faith and love, among the highest of Christian virtues (13:11). As he wrote in his epistle to the Romans, "[W]e also boast in our sufferings, knowing that suffering produces endurance, and endurance produces character, and character produces hope, and hope does not disappoint us, because God's love has been poured into our hearts through the Holy Spirit that has been given to us" (5:3–5).

As Paul uses it in his epistles, the word *hope* does not refer to a vague wish, but to the confident expectation of a good future with God. When Paul talks about hope, then, he is not talking about the sort of wishful thinking that a child has when she or he hopes to get a certain present for Christmas. Instead, hope means that we have a genuine expectation and anticipation that something will happen, such as when we look forward with hope and confident anticipation that Christmas will come on December twenty-fifth each year, and that we will be able to celebrate with friends and family. The blessed hope and confident expectation of Christians is that in the end God will be in charge. God will rule—through the work of Jesus Christ.

It is important to note that, in the New Testament, hope in what is to come is never given as a reason to be complacent today. Instead, hope is offered as a motivation for being persistent in our service to God. Some Christians are so concerned about future events that it paralyzes them from acting out their faith in the present. In the first epistle to the Thessalonians, the church at Thessalonica was encouraged to have hope in the future. From reading the Second Letter to the Thessalonians, however, it appears as though members of the church were quitting their jobs and just sitting around thinking about

Christ's return. They were ignoring their work on Earth. In response to this, the epistle charges them in no uncertain terms to stop being idle and get back to work (3:6–10).

Our hope does not call us to dwell in the future and contemplate heavenly things while neglecting our mission here on Earth. Our hope calls us to be concerned with real issues here and now—like disease, death, and injustice—rather than dwelling on future prophecies and waiting for God to take us away from it all. Our hope that God will reign should motivate us to work for God's purposes today, because we know that there is a bright light at the end of the tunnel. Like the heroes of today's fantasy stories, our hope should inspire us to be even more committed to our quests now. To do otherwise would be to prove Karl Marx right: our religion really does become the opium of the people.[1]

In our personal life, our hope in a future with God can give us strength when we hit the rough sections of the road. Psychologists tell us that depression can come when we feel that our lives are hopeless and we see no way out. As Christians, we know that life is never hopeless, and that with God things can and will get better. We might not see a way out today, but we just may be able to see it tomorrow. When we are feeling hopeless, we can seek out ministers and church members who, like Samwise Gamgee, can encourage us and give us hope of finding a way out. When our faith journey takes us through dark places, our hope in God can serve as a beacon of light, so we can see the way out. When we feel like our spirits are fading, our hope can work like a magnet that pulls us through to the other side.

The Road Goes Ever On: Life after Life

Myths and legends throughout the ages have explored the human longing for immortality. Death is a reality for all people, but mythic figures going as far back as Gilgamesh the King have tried to find ways to cheat death. One of the hardest times in life is when we must cope with the death of a loved one or face our own mortality. We have a heartfelt desire to know that the years we have on earth are not all there is.

Although all three of today's popular fantasy stories deal with the reality of death, they also allude to some kind of afterlife. Harry Potter sees magical manifestations of his parents in the Mirror of Erised in *Harry Potter and the Sorcerer's Stone*, in the Patronus he conjures in

Harry Potter and the Prisoner of Azkaban, and from Voldemort's wand in *Harry Potter and the Goblet of Fire.* These images let him know that somehow, in some way, his parents still exist. But, as Harry learns in *Harry Potter and the Order of the Phoenix,* he cannot know exactly what awaits his loved ones "beyond the veil."[2]

In *Return of the Jedi,* even the nine-hundred-year-old Yoda eventually dies. But in the *Star Wars* universe, at least for Jedi, death apparently is not the end. After his death, Obi-Wan Kenobi repeatedly appears in spirit form to guide Luke. At the end of *Return of the Jedi,* Obi-Wan, Yoda, and Anakin Skywalker are all visibly present during the closing celebrations. In *Attack of the Clones,* Cliegg Lars demonstrates hope that his wife, Shmi, lives on in some way after her death. At her graveside he says, "I know wherever you are, it's become a better place."

In *The Two Towers,* Frodo and Sam get disturbing glimpses of faces in the mysterious Dead Marshes. In *The Return of the King,* Aragorn leads his riders through the Paths of the Dead, and there is joined by the Dead, who need to fulfill an oath in order to find rest. In both instances much is left unexplained about the nature of the dead.

One of the primary hopes for many Christians is the hope of life after death. But in a manner similar to the fantasy stories described above, the Bible does not provide many details concerning the nature of life after death. According to the Gospel of Mark, the Sadducees presented Jesus with a hypothetical situation in which a woman is widowed and then marries her deceased husband's brother. That brother dies, so the woman marries yet another brother, and so on, until she has been married to seven brothers from the same family. The Sadducees then ask Jesus, "In the resurrection whose wife will she be?" (Mark 12:23). Jesus' answer does not give us a clear image of the afterlife, except to say that in the resurrection, people "neither marry nor are given in marriage" (Mark 12:25). Jesus' terse reply suggests two things. First, his answer assures us of some kind of life after this life. Second, it presumes that that life will not be like our life on earth. It is significant that Jesus concludes his thoughts on the subject by saying that God is not the God of the dead, but of the living (Mark 12:27).

Christians' belief in eternal life has historically led them to defend the dignity and value of all life. Throughout the history of the church, Christians have opposed the attitude that human life is cheap and disposable. The early church provided pagans with Christian burials rather than let their bodies be disposed of as though they were garbage. In later centuries members of the church became forceful advocates for human rights in a variety of societies and cultures around the world. As individuals, a belief in the eternal life of humankind leads us to value our own life and to value the lives of those around us. We may not be given details on the nature of life after death, but regardless of the details, the prospect of eternal life is truly an awesome one.

Although today's fantasy stories may express vague images of an afterlife, they are much clearer in their attitude toward those who jealously hang onto their earthly life at any cost. In *Harry Potter and the Order of the Phoenix,* the ghost Nearly Headless Nick confides to Harry that he feared death, but now regrets choosing a "feeble imitation of life"[3] over it. In *Harry Potter and the Sorcerer's Stone,* Lord Voldemort tries to extend his life by artificial means. First, he kills a pure and innocent unicorn and drinks its magical blood. It is a desperate measure on his part. We are told that drinking unicorn blood will only extend one's life as a kind of ongoing half-life. Second, Voldemort seeks the sorcerer's stone so that he can make the Elixir of Life, which will cause him to live forever. Not surprisingly, Professor Dumbledore takes a very different approach to death. He tells Harry that death is not something that needs to be avoided at all costs, but that "to the well-organized mind, death is but the next great adventure."[4]

In *Attack of the Clones,* Anakin cannot accept his mother's death. His inability to deal with her mortality is a turning point in his life. His defiant pledge, "I will even learn to stop people from dying," is a sign that he is slipping into the Dark Side.

In *The Lord of the Rings,* the One Ring has the power to extend life artificially. The ring bearer Gollum lives for ages because of the Ring. But the source of Gollum's extended life has twisted him both physically and emotionally. Bilbo Baggins barely ages while he holds the Ring. He does not feel old, but he says that he feels spread out and thin. When the time comes for Bilbo to give up the Ring, he understands that it is better for him to live out his life more naturally, and eventually to sail off into the sunset.

In the Gospel of Luke, Jesus teaches his followers: "[T]hose who want to save their life will lose it, and those who lose their life for my sake will save it. What does it profit them if they gain the whole world, but lose or forfeit themselves?" (9:24–25). The context of Jesus' words make it clear that he was, at least in part, speaking to his disciples about losing their physical lives. He was telling his disciples that as valuable as this life is, other things are even more valuable. At some point they need to be willing to let it go.

Many people today have an unnatural fixation on staying young in appearance and extending life through artificial means. Belief in the value and dignity of life should lead Christians to value their health and to use available medical means to extend life when it is possible and appropriate, but it should also help us recognize and accept when it is time to let go. Many families, for example, have found that good hospice care is more life affirming than using extraordinary means to prolong life with little prospect of extending the quality of life.

For most of us, the death of a loved one is one of the most difficult times of our lives. Although Christians still mourn the death of people they love, they do "not grieve as others do who have no hope" (1 Thess. 4:13). Believing in eternal life does not mean that we are not sorry about death, but it does mean that we have hope that God is there, even beyond the limits of this life. In the First Letter of Paul to the Corinthians, he argues that Christ's resurrection conquered the power of death, and that while death is an end, it is not *the* end (1 Cor. 15).

According to the Gospel of John, Jesus said, "[A]nyone who hears my words and believes him who sent me has eternal life" (5:24). By putting this comment in the present tense, Jesus' words suggest that our eternal life is something that starts now. What does the future hold? Will we be walking around with others in heaven? Will we see and know our loved ones? Though the Bible gives us a number of intriguing images to work with, it does not clearly spell out the details. Some people claim to have near-death experiences, but no one has come up with a scientifically verifiable description of the life to come. Many questions are left unanswered. Like so many of life's questions, the complete answer lies in the mystery of our faith.

At the end of *Harry Potter and the Goblet of Fire,* Albus Dumbledore attempts to prepare his students for those times "when you have to make a choice between what is right and what is easy."[5] Our faith journey will inevitably call us to choose some rough roads. During these difficult times, we will need to demonstrate perseverance. We must keep moving forward in our faith even when we do not feel like it. Our hope in the ultimate goodness of God can pull us through the darkest of times and motivate us to action.

Questions for Reflection

Today's fantasy stories feature many rough roads and seemingly hopeless situations. Which one is the most memorable to you? How did the heroes find their way out of the situation?

To use the metaphor of this chapter, what are some of the "roughest roads" that you have had to travel?

Have you ever had to be persistent in your faith even when you did not feel like it?

How has God helped you make it through your roughest times?

How does your hope affect your life?

What do you believe the afterlife will be like? How does your belief in life after death affect the way you live today?

The Trail of Trials: Our Internal and External Battles

When I was a young child, I slipped away from my house, grabbed a fallen branch as a walking stick, and set off on an adventure. I walked through an open field and arrived at the beginning of a narrow pathway set between the edge of a forested hill and an overgrown swamp. The pathway was shadowed by a thick growth of trees, so it was dark and foreboding even in the middle of the day. But I took off on the path anyway. The branches of the trees were twisted and eerie. Strange noises (what I later learned were the chirps and croaks of many frogs) came from the swamp. I was scared, but I gripped my stick tighter and kept going so that I could see where the path led. I was rewarded for my perseverance. The other side of the dark path opened up into a beautiful sunlit clearing filled with green grass, beautiful trees, wildflowers, and butterflies. To my young eyes, it looked like a secret paradise hidden from the rest of the world by the thick forest and swamp that bordered it on all sides. I returned home thrilled with my discovery.

Even at such a young age, my journeys to this place and back home again had a profound effect on me. They helped me understand a bit more about the world around my home, and having made it through the dark pathway and back, I even learned a bit more about myself and what I was capable of doing. I did not know it at the time, but I was not alone in my feelings about such a journey. In a small way, I had reenacted the sort of mythic journey that people have been finding meaningful for ages.

To succeed in our journeys, we must move through many dark and foreboding pathways and face many trials. Scholars of ancient myths and legends have identified several recurring motifs in the hero's journey, including passing through a mysterious forest, dealing with parents, descending into a watery abyss, entering a labyrinth, and slaying a dragon. These recurring stages on the hero's journey are sometimes referred to as "the trail of trials."[1] According to many scholars of mythology, ancient storytellers, consciously or quite unconsciously, used these aspects of the journey to symbolize the internal and external struggles that people face in their spiritual lives. A wide variety of psychological and sociological interpretations have been given for the meaning of each of these motifs.

The ancient Greek myth of Theseus serves as a helpful example of the use of these motifs and how they function in myths. As a young man, just coming of age, Theseus begins his trail of trials by traveling the dangerous isthmus road from Troezen to Athens. On the path he meets and defeats six murderous robbers, including Periphetes, the club-man; Sinis, the pine-bender; Phaia, the Crommyonian sow; Sciron and his man-eating turtle; and Procrustes and his deadly magic bed. This isthmus road is not literally a road through a mysterious forest, but it functions in much the same way. Theseus braves this frightening pathway and the mysterious creatures that dwell along it, and makes it through to the other side. In so doing he gains confidence in himself and is emboldened to go further on his journey.

Theseus also must deal with his parents. Dealing with the issues of parenting is often an important step in the hero's journey. Theseus's adoptive father, King Aegeus of Athens, loves him more than life itself. But when Theseus arrives in Crete, he boldly proclaims to King Minos that he is the son of Poseidon, god of the sea. Minos, however, expresses his doubts. To prove to Minos that he has Poseidon's favor, Theseus dives into a watery abyss. He is escorted by a school of dolphins and, at the bottom of the sea receives a crown and a golden ring from Amphitrite, goddess of the sea. These special gifts are a visible sign that he has found favor with the gods. By diving into the abyss and returning, the hero is able to claim his identity and is further emboldened for the task before him.

Theseus is perhaps best known for entering into a labyrinth, a complicated maze, to face the Minotaur. Once every nine years, King Minos of Crete demanded a tribute from Athens of seven young men and seven young women. These young people would be thrown into the labyrinth to be eaten by the monster known as the Minotaur, who lived in its depths. Theseus determines to end this injustice by facing the Minotaur. He poses as one of the sacrificial victims. Instead of trying to hide and escape the evil within, Theseus valiantly seeks out the Minotaur. By boldly entering into a labyrinth to face a force of evil, the hero shows great bravery and commitment to the mission at hand. The Minotaur, a vicious man-eating creature who is half-man and half-bull, functions as the dragon in the story. It is an evil threat, not only to Theseus but also to others in his world. Theseus slays the Minotaur, and then helps the other young people escape from the labyrinth. By slaying the dragon, the hero has faced and conquered evil in the world and helped others in the process. When Theseus returns home (another common mythic motif that will be explored in chapter 12), he has to deal with more issues. Theseus's own thoughtlessness is the cause of his stepfather King Aegeus's death. Theseus is crushed by this realization, and for a time ends up following in his stepfather's footsteps as a king. But according to some myths, Theseus later makes his own way in the world as a wandering adventurer.

There are more recurring motifs in the "trail of trials" than are mentioned in this chapter, and this chapter does not offer a comprehensive survey of all possible interpretations of their meaning. Instead, it looks at some of the ways these motifs function in the Harry Potter stories, the *Star Wars* films, and *The Lord of the Rings* trilogy, and draws connections to the ways the same themes are explored in the Bible. As we reflect on this trail of trials, we are challenged to look closely at our own lives, and therefore be better prepared for our own journey.

Into the Mysterious Forest: Facing the Unknown in Our World and Ourselves

In myths and fairy tales, forests are places that are full of unknown dangers and supernatural forces. Although heroes would rather avoid the mysterious dark forest, their paths often take them straight through the heart of it. Many scholars see these forests as symbols, representing the dark recesses of our unconscious mind and the mysterious aspects of the world in which we live.[2] When heroes enter the dark forest, they are courageously facing the unknown. By successfully completing this part of their journey and emerging on the other side of the forest, they grow confident in their ability to face the unknown in the future.

Today's fantasy stories each contain several scenes that carry on this mythic forest motif. In *Harry Potter and the Sorcerer's Stone,* the students at Hogwarts are strictly prohibited from entering the nearby Forbidden Forest, which is said to be home to many mysterious and deadly creatures. As part of a detention he has earned, Harry must enter the Forbidden Forest in search of an injured unicorn. He faces great danger and confronts several mysterious creatures. One of these, a centaur named Firenze, grants Harry the rare privilege of riding on his back and warns him of the grave danger that he faces. In *Harry Potter and the Chamber of Secrets,* both Harry and Ron must return to the Forbidden Forest. This trip is especially challenging for Ron, who must face his fear of spiders in order to help his friend Hagrid. Following a hint from Hagrid, Ron and Harry follow a path of small spiders in search of the answer to a mystery. Ron's worst nightmare is realized when he comes face to face with a family of giant spiders who try to eat him. When Ron and Harry escape and emerge from the forest, they have learned more about their own characters and the mysteries of their world. What is more, they have gained confidence in their ability to carry out the mission before them.

In *The Empire Strikes Back,* Luke Skywalker enters a forested swamp world in the Dagobah system. It is there that Yoda challenges Luke to understand the spiritual nature of the world around him, and to understand himself better as well. When Luke enters into the tree cave, he does not know what dangerous mystery awaits him. By facing the unknown, he learns a painful but valuable truth about himself.

The forests of Middle-earth function in a similar manner. They contain dangers and mysteries, but they also lead to greater understanding. In *The Hobbit,* Bilbo Baggins's path takes him through the heart of Mirkwood forest. As he makes his way through the forest, Bilbo discovers that the world is even more dangerous than he had thought. He learns a great deal about himself and his mettle. He faces wood-elves and giant spiders and realizes that he is capable of triumphing over them. He comes to understand his dwarf companions better as well, and once they are through the forest, he no longer feels inferior to them. Bilbo's journey through Mirkwood is a frightening experience to be sure, but it gives him great confidence for the future.

In the forest of Lothlórien, in *The Fellowship of the Ring,* Lady Galadriel looks into the minds and hearts of the members of the Fellowship and makes them confront things about themselves that they would rather not see. Sam admits to feeling naked under her stare. Each member of the Fellowship reacts differently to the test of the Lady's gaze. Some face their fears, others their weaknesses. Still others are able to recognize their inner strengths. Galadriel's stare prods them to take a troubling but enlightening look at themselves and the tasks that lie before them.

It is human nature to fear the mysterious forests of our lives. Facing uncertainty can be especially difficult for those who expect their religion to provide certainty about every aspect of life. Jesus' disciples stepped into an unknown future when they dropped everything to follow him. They could not have foreseen all the dangers along the way. Huddled together between that first Good Friday and the first Easter morning, they must have faced one of the darkest times in their lives. It was likely a time of fear and doubt, when they had to look both outward at the world around them and deep inside themselves to discover who they truly were and what they truly believed.

The Christian faith teaches us that we live in mystery, and that we must come to accept that we do not know the future. According to the Gospel of Matthew, Jesus taught that we must accept that God knows the future and we do not (6:34, 24:36). The Christian faith does not promise us certainty, but it does promise us the strength to live with uncertainty. As the Psalmist wrote, "Even though I walk through the darkest valley, I fear no evil; for you are with me; your rod and your staff—they comfort me" (23:4).

We do not know what dangers await us when we enter unfamiliar territory. But by traveling to new places, seeking new experiences, meeting new types of people, or jumping into a challenging job, we learn more about ourselves and the world around us. In addition, our trips into the unknown give us confidence to successfully deal with whatever might come our way. Our faith journey is not all about playing it safe and staying within our comfort zones. To move ahead in the journey, at times we must travel through a mysterious forest.

Dealing with Dad (and Mom)

When we take a long, hard look at ourselves, some of the issues we confront have to do with our relationship with our parents. Our fantasy heroes are no different from the rest of us in this respect; some of their deepest personal concerns revolve around unresolved issues with their parents.

Every one of the Harry Potter stories deals with this issue. Harry is an orphan whose parents were killed by Lord Voldemort when he was just one year old. In *Harry Potter and the Sorcerer's Stone,* Harry stands before the Mirror of Eristed, an enchanted mirror that reflects back to him an image of his deepest heart's desire—his parents standing beside him. Harry would gladly spend days on end looking at their image in the mirror. Harry endures many insults and abuse at school and at home without losing his temper, but he really gets angry when someone insults the memory of his parents. Throughout the stories Harry is confronted with supernatural visitations by his parents. In Harry's case, despite his sorrow these visitations give him a greater sense of who he is and who he wants to be. When he makes a connection with his parents and senses their love for him, he gains strength for the trials that he must face on his journey.

Luke Skywalker has perhaps the most troubling father figure of all. Assuming himself to be an orphan, Luke is confronted with the fact that his father is alive and that he is Darth Vader, a Jedi Knight who turned to the Dark Side. When he first learns this information about his father, Luke is in denial. Through the Force, Luke senses that Vader truly is his father, but his heart refuses to accept it. Over time Luke comes to grips with the truth, and is able to accept part of his father's heritage as his own. Near the end of *The Return of the Jedi,* in the midst of their battle, Luke defiantly tells the Emperor, "I am a Jedi, like my father before me." Luke takes an amazing stance. He does not ignore his father's evil deeds or submit to his abuse. He refuses to be like his father and continues to fight against Vader's cause. But he also tries to redeem the father who abandoned him and who has caused him such pain. He does not yield to his father's evil ways or try to repay evil with evil. Instead, he tries to overcome his father's acts of evil with acts of good.

In *Attack of the Clones,* Anakin Skywalker is less successful in dealing with issues surrounding his parents. He loves his mother, but has not visited her in years. When she dies, he does not deal well with his grief. Instead, he lashes out against others. He resorts to brutal vengeance that turns into indiscriminate slaughter. Anakin grew up without a father, but he tells Padmé that his mentor Obi-Wan Kenobi is "like my father." Anakin cannot deal with having to answer to Obi-Wan. Instead of dealing with the tensions, Anakin lets his anger toward Obi-Wan grow until, as we see in *Star Wars: A New Hope,* he eventually kills Obi-Wan and leaves himself that much more detached from his own humanity.

Frodo Baggins lost his father and mother at a young age, and was raised by his uncle Bilbo. This has clearly been a loving relationship, and the two deeply miss each other when the time comes, in *The Fellowship of the Ring*, for them to part. Bilbo leaves the Ring with Frodo. When they meet again, Bilbo asks to see the Ring, and for a horrifying moment, Bilbo fiercely demands that Frodo give it back to him, demonstrating that even a good relationship can become strained when a possession is involved. Bilbo and Frodo are able to talk and voice their love for each other and express their regrets about the way their lives and their relationship turned out. Frodo struggles with how much he is like Bilbo and how he is different from Bilbo as well. In the end Frodo realizes that he needs to find his own way in the world.

It is no coincidence that the parent-child relationship plays such a key role in these three stories; it is a common theme in stories that deal with spiritual issues. The Gospels tell us about some of Jesus' issues with his parents. According to the Gospel of John, there was tension between Jesus and his mother, Mary, at a wedding they attended in Cana. Mary, perhaps to push Jesus to accept his calling, urges him to turn water into wine when the wine at the wedding runs out. At first Jesus resists and says to his mother: "Woman, what concern is that to you and to me? My hour has not yet come" (2:4). But Mary tells the servants to follow Jesus' instructions. We are told that Jesus relented and performed his first miracle by doing what Mary asked him to do. According to the Gospel of Mark, there came a time later in his ministry when it became clear that Jesus had identified his own mission apart from his family of origin. When Jesus is told that his mother, brothers, and sisters had arrived, he looks at those who are sitting around him and says: "Here are my mother and my brothers! Whoever does the will of God is my brother and sister and mother" (3:34–35).

At the very end of his life, the Gospel of John tells us that Jesus was concerned for his mother's welfare. Even as he suffered on the cross, Jesus made sure that "the disciple whom he loved" would look after Mary and take her into his home (19:26–27).

The Gospel of Matthew explores issues between Father and Son as Jesus struggles in Gethsemane before his betrayal and crucifixion. In his grief he addresses his prayer to "My Father" (26:36–46), though others taunt him for calling himself "God's Son" (27:40, 43). His final cry of anguish on the cross, "My God, my God, why have you forsaken me?" (27:46), expresses the pain of a child abandoned by a parent.

When we speak of God as Father today, it is important that we remember that this is one of many images of God that the Bible gives to us. Christians often pray, "Our Father, who art in heaven," but they are rarely exposed to other images of God. Some Christians therefore can make the mistake of believing that the God whom the Bible calls spirit (John 4:24), a consuming fire (Heb. 12:29), light (1 John 1:5), and love (1 John 4:16) is somehow a male parent much like their own. Thankfully, the Bible gives us a wide range of images for God. These include masculine images, such as a wrestler (Gen. 32:22–32) and a shepherd (Isa. 40:11), as well as feminine images, such as a mother (Hos. 11:1–4) and a woman cleaning house (Luke 15:8–10). The Scriptures also use animal imagery to describe God, such as a dove (Matt. 3:16–17) and an eagle (Exod. 19:3–6), and even images of inanimate objects, such as a rock (Ps. 62:1–2, Isa. 51:1–3). We cannot talk about the infinite God as though any one word or image could capture God's full essence. If we were to do so, we would be limiting God and therefore guilty of idolatry. Everyone will find images of God that are more helpful than others. But the wide variety of images of God can help us reflect on the many aspects of the nature of God.

For many Christians, the image of God as Father is a helpful one. It challenges us to reflect on a God who gives us life, comforts us, cares for us, and gives us what we need. It can also help us reflect on the image of a parent who stands over us, and whom we are told to honor and obey. But people who have had unpleasant relationships with their earthly parents may choose to use other biblical images of God in their prayers and devotional reflections.

In *Harry Potter and the Order of the Phoenix,* Harry must deal with the realization that neither his father nor his godfather was perfect. Yet he still loves them and honors them. In our faith journeys, we are called on to deal with issues surrounding our earthly parents and to take a realistic look at our relationships with them. We may need to ask ourselves how we can honor our parents (Eph. 6:2), while at the same time honestly acknowledging that they are not perfect and may have even "provoked [us] to anger" (Eph. 6:4). These are issues that can linger for a lifetime. Some may find it helpful to speak to a counselor or a minister to work through issues of guilt, anger, or loss surrounding these relationships. Often we need to work through issues surrounding our parents if we are to move forward on our faith journey.

Descending into the Abyss: Going to the Depths to Find Ourselves

When heroes descend into the depths of an abyss, it can be taken as a metaphor for going deep inside themselves. Through their journeys into the depths, heroes discover something new about their identity and their place in the world, and they emerge with a new sense of self.

In *Harry Potter and the Goblet of Fire,* a friend or relative of each champion competing in the Triwizard Tournament is taken hostage by Merpeople and tied up at the bottom of the lake at Hogwarts. The task of each of the four champions is to descend into the lake, overcome the dangers that lurk there, retrieve their hostage, and return the hostage to the surface in less than an hour. Harry reaches his hostage, Ron, in plenty of time. But instead of rushing back to win the race, Harry stays behind to make sure that all four people are rescued. In the process of descending into the depths of the lake and ascending again, Harry learns some things about himself. He learns that he may be naïve about the nature of such contests (Dumbledore would never allow the four hostages in this contest to be in any real danger), but he also proves to himself and to others that he has moral fiber.

In *Star Wars: A New Hope,* Luke Skywalker, Han Solo, Leia Organa, and Chewbacca go into the depths of the Death Star. Ultimately they work themselves into its very core and end up in its giant, watery trash compactor. This experience reveals the heroes' character: Han, Leia, and Luke bicker and complain, even when they are at the core of the Death Star. It takes Obi-Wan's sacrifice to challenge them to reflect on the gravity of the mission before them when they finally emerge.

In *The Phantom Menace,* when Jar Jar Binks descends through the lake into the depths of Naboo with Qui-Gon Jinn and Obi-Wan Kenobi, he is going back home. But even for Jar Jar, the journey into the abyss is a discovery of who he is. If he stays there, he faces death. Instead, he emerges from the depths with the Jedi and takes his first steps toward a new mission for his life.

In the Gospels, the ultimate story of descending into the depths is the story of Jesus, who died, "descended into the lower parts of the earth" (Eph. 4:9), and emerged to new life. This story will be explored in some detail in the next chapter.

Baptism provides another biblical image of watery descent and ascent. Jesus' baptism was a turning point for him and his ministry. When he enters public ministry, Jesus is baptized by John the Baptist, descending into the water and emerging to hear the voice of God saying, "This is my Son, the Beloved, with whom I am well pleased" (Matt. 3:17). After Jesus receives this declaration of his identity, he journeys off into the desert to prepare for his mission.

The ancient rite of baptism plays on the imagery of descending into and emerging from the abyss. Those who are baptized symbolically die to their old lives and are symbolically buried by going underwater. They emerge from their watery grave as a sign that they are reborn into a new life. Paul alludes to this symbolism when he writes, "Therefore we have been buried with him by baptism into death, so that, just as Christ was raised from the dead by the glory of the Father, so we too might walk in newness of life" (Rom. 6:4). This act of baptism, descending into the water and emerging to new life, is a powerful image that is still practiced in many Christian traditions today. It is the way people publicly proclaim to the world their identity as Christians.

Joseph Campbell explores this motif of the abyss through the story of Jonah and the whale. Jonah's physical experience of going into the belly of the whale is parallel to his spiritual experience. He looks inward, which leads him to prayer, repentance, and praise of God (Jon. 2). As Campbell puts it, "the hero goes inward, to be born again."[3]

At times in our faith journey, we are also called to dive into the abyss in order to claim our identity. We are asked to look honestly and deeply at who we are and what we have done in our life. We may need to deal with the way we have hurt people or the times we have been unfaithful. We may need to deal with personal issues of loss, such as the death of a loved one, the loss of a relationship, a disappointment or a rejection, or becoming a victim of a crime or a natural disaster. Many people find it helpful to meet with a counselor or a minister to help them talk through their difficult times. If we continue to ignore issues, then we can become stalled in our faith journeys. If we have the courage to face these issues head-on, however, we will be taking the first steps toward profound growth in our life. The good news is that many people find that they emerge from the abyss like Jonah, strengthened and changed for the better. They have a stronger sense of self and are better able to embrace their identity as a person of faith.

Unfortunately, some people of faith feel guilty about taking the time to look inward. They feel that being a person of faith means that we should not admit to having any problems or struggles in our personal lives. As a matter of fact, some Christians may be in danger of using their religion and Church life to avoid facing personal issues or problems with others. But we need to face these issues honestly and head-on to better understand ourselves and our world. We need to look inward and grow personally in order to help the world around us.

Entering the Labyrinth: Facing Evil with No Turning Back

The journey into a labyrinth is a journey into the depths of a complex maze. Heroes enter the labyrinth knowing they will have to confront evil and danger at its center, and that once they begin their journey, they will not find any easy way out. The step into the labyrinth is a step of uncompromising commitment to the task at hand and a step of great courage.

This is a recurring motif that serves as the climax of the Harry Potter stories. In *Harry Potter and the Sorcerer's Stone,* Harry must overcome a maze of obstacles in order to descend into the depths of Hogwarts and face a deadly wizard. In *Harry Potter and the Chamber of Secrets,* Harry descends into the chamber to rescue a friend. In *Harry Potter and the Prisoner of Azkaban,* Harry travels the maze of hidden tunnels beneath Hogwarts to face a dangerous wizard who is out to kill him. For the final task of the Triwizard Tournament, in *Harry Potter and the Goblet of Fire,* Harry enters a labyrinth of many dangers; even he is unaware of the full measure of the danger when he enters it. At the conclusion of *Harry Potter and the Order of the Phoenix,* Harry leads his friends into the depths of the Ministry of

Magic, navigating a maze of rooms and doorways in order to confront the Evil One. Harry must take these journeys in order to win the battle, but they also serve as tests of his character. The Harry Potter books are, among other things, coming-of-age stories. Part of the way Harry grows up is by facing his fears and confronting the Evil One.

In *Star Wars: A New Hope,* Luke Skywalker enters the labyrinth of the exterior of the Death Star. He must negotiate the maze in his ship, while flying at top speed in order to successfully complete his mission. When he sets aside his targeting device, he embraces who he is and his place in the universe, and affirms his confidence in himself and in the Force. This theme is developed even further in *Return of the Jedi.* Luke descends into the depths of the second Death Star, knowing that he will have to face evil in the form of Darth Vader. Vader poses not only a physical threat but also an emotional and spiritual threat, for Luke is aware that Vader is his father. Luke knows the danger he will find there, and yet he still enters the Death Star. He knows that it is his destiny; he knows that he must make a stand.

In *The Phantom Menace,* the young Padawan apprentice Obi-Wan Kenobi follows his master Qui-Gon Jinn into a labyrinth of catwalks in a power generator to face the evil and deadly Darth Maul. Walls of deadly rays suddenly form behind the heroes, cutting off their retreat, or in front of them, cutting off their progress. Darth Maul is a powerful and frightening enemy, but Qui-Gon and Obi-Wan bravely leap into harm's way to destroy the evil Darth Maul. When Obi-Wan is momentarily cut off from the battle by a wall of rays, he watches helplessly as Darth Maul brutally kills Qui-Gon. Instead of making a hasty retreat, Obi-Wan leaps into the battle the next chance he gets. He understands that as a Jedi he has a duty to confront the evil before him.

In *The Fellowship of the Ring,* the Mines of Moria hold many dangers in their dark and twisting pathways. Readers of the novel and viewers of the film are given hints that Gandalf knows if he enters the Mines of Moria, there is a good chance he will never emerge from them. He knows of the Evil One, the Balrog, that dwells in Moria's depths. He does not wish to enter Moria and tries to lead the Fellowship in another direction. But when they meet an impasse, he leads them through the mines' labyrinth of pathways. When the time comes, Gandalf does not hesitate to face the evil that lurks there.

The quest of Frodo Baggins and Sam Gamgee takes them through many winding and narrow passages into the very heart of Mordor and Mount Doom itself. They cannot avoid what they fear.

They must enter into the shadow of the Evil One, Sauron, to succeed in their mission. They hold firm to their faith, hope, and commitment to their cause, and continue forward on their quest.

In the Gospels, the desert functions as a labyrinth of sorts. At first consideration the openness of a desert might not seem much like a labyrinth. But in Jesus' day, the desert was considered a mysterious and dangerous place. Once someone entered the desert—where nearly every stretch of land and rock formation looked the same—they could easily become lost and never find their way out. When a person entered the desert, they were leaving behind everything that was comfortable and familiar and entering a world of danger. Jesus enters the desert knowing the dangers that wait for him. But the Spirit leads him to that place in order to face the Evil One and be tempted by him (Matt. 4:1–11). Jesus endures the devil's temptations and stands firm in his faith. When he emerges from the desert, he is ready to call his disciples and take the next steps in his own journey.

According to the Gospel of Matthew, when Jesus told his disciples that he had to go to Jerusalem, they were understandably afraid of what awaited them there. Jesus knew that by going to Jerusalem, he would have to confront the evils of sin and death (16:21–26). But Jesus did not sneak into Jerusalem. He entered it in a very public way on that first Palm Sunday, to the cheers and acclaim of many people. Once he entered Jerusalem in this manner, he knew there would be no turning back. But Jesus did not hesitate and entered Jerusalem prepared to confront the evil before him. Jesus feared the cross, but was committed to following his mission to it.

Throughout the ages Christians have followed their calling into dangerous places and confronted the evil before them. They have knowingly risked their livelihoods, their reputations, and even their physical safety by entering into the labyrinths of the world and courageously facing evil. Some gave up their lives in the quest. Their rebirth is with God. Others made it through these trials and have found themselves profoundly changed by their experiences.

Slaying Dragons: Changing the World with Tangible Results

When the hero enters the labyrinth, it is often a dragon or other monster that she or he must face. In today's fantasy tales, the heroes face actual dragons, including Norbert, in *Harry Potter and the Sorcerer's Stone*, and Smaug, who is slain by Bard the Bowman in *The Hobbit.*

However, in this section the phrase "slaying dragons" is used as a metaphor for an action that accomplishes concrete good in the world or that overcomes something evil or unjust. Many who study myths explore the motif of slaying dragons as a symbol of one's inner struggles and personal triumphs. But when ancient heroes such as Theseus defeated dragons and monsters, they were also taking concrete steps to rid the world of evil and help those around them. Slaying dragons is a concrete action with lasting external results.

The journeys of Harry Potter, Luke Skywalker, and Frodo Baggins were not only times of self-discovery and personal growth, they also served to defeat evil in a concrete way. The triumphs of these heroes provided help for others and made their world a better place. Harry Potter learns about himself in his battles with his nemesis Voldemort, but he also holds off Voldemort's rise to power over the wizarding world. In so doing he is not only helping himself but also making a far-reaching contribution to his world.

The Death Star functions as the dragon to be slain in *Star Wars: A New Hope.* Through his adventures Luke Skywalker not only learns about the spiritual nature of the universe in which he lives, he also accomplishes something that helps others in a concrete way. When he blows up the Death Star, it is a major setback for the oppressive Empire.

In *The Lord of the Rings,* Frodo wears his dragon—the One Ring—on a chain around his neck. His effort to destroy the Ring is an attempt to destroy the power of Sauron and prevent him from taking over Middle-earth. In the process Frodo learns a great deal about himself, but he is also striving to help his world.

It is fitting that the Book of Revelation uses the image of casting the dragon into the abyss to illustrate Christ's victory over evil (Rev. 20:1–3). Christians believe that Jesus' journey to the cross, death, burial, and resurrection, did more than just help Jesus learn about himself, his world, and his God. In some mysterious way, Jesus Christ's death and resurrection conquered the power of sin and death.

Jesus himself had little patience for those whose faith journey was egocentric, lived out for personal justification or fulfillment. Jesus demanded that one's faith be demonstrated by how one treated and cared for others, especially those in need (Matt. 25:31–46). The writers of the epistles told the early Church that their faith must be evidenced in how they care for others (James 2:14–26, 1 John 4:19–21). According to the epistle of James, "Religion that is pure and undefiled before God, the Father, is this: to care for orphans and widows in their distress, and to keep oneself unstained by the world" (1:27).

Although it is important for us to look inward at the issues that may be holding us back on our faith journey, it is also crucial that we look outward at the state of the world and the plight of our neighbors. In the western world, religion tends to be egocentric. People practice their faith to gain a sense of self-fulfillment and self-actualization. Many churches focus most of their programs and much of their budgets on serving their members, so that they understand Christianity and understand themselves. These are noble goals, but according to the Christian faith, we need to look outward and put our faith into action. We need to look around us and help people who are lonely, starving, suffering under oppression, struggling with disease, and facing death.

Many towns and cities have several small churches of the same denomination that are all struggling. Instead of merging these churches, they stay separated and commit their time and money to paying separate pastors and keeping their separate buildings up and running. Rather than staying apart for the sake of their own comfort and fulfillment, they would do well to consider joining their resources so they can better reach out into their communities. In this way they can devote time, money, and energy to the people and problems that exist outside the doors of their churches. They can focus their resources on slaying the dragons of their community and their world.

It is important to note that our heroes do not expect to obliterate evil completely as they take on their dangerous quests. When Harry defeats Voldemort, he does not completely rid the world of him. At the end of *Harry Potter and the Prisoner of Azkaban,* Harry feels that he has made no difference at all because he was unable to accomplish all that he set out to do. Professor Dumbledore, however, reminds Harry of the good that he has done, and that for particular people, he has made all the difference in the world.

In *Star Wars: A New Hope,* when Luke Skywalker blows up the Death Star, he knows that he has not destroyed the Empire; he has just destroyed their most powerful weapon. Luke understands that his action is just one act in a greater cause. The eventual creation of a new Death Star does not diminish the value of Luke's destruction of the first one.

When Frodo Baggins sets out to destroy the Ring, he is attempting to destroy the power of Sauron. This is a great cause in and of itself. But we learn that destroying Sauron's power does not obliterate evil from Middle-earth. Evil outlasts the Ring.

In the same way, while Christians believe that Christ's death and resurrection defeated the power of sin and death, they also recognize that sin and death are still active in the world, and that they must do all that they can to resist it. Like the heroes of the fantasy stories, we may follow a calling that does not conclude with a perfect ending. We might volunteer at a soup kitchen, yet be overwhelmed when we realize that we will never totally obliterate hunger in the world. Still, we can take some solace in knowing that we are helping some people in the process. We may work hard to enact just public policies, only to find our cause defeated in a legislative decision or public election. But we can encourage ourselves with the thought that we are helping to keep the public debate more balanced than it would be without our voice. We may be discouraged to find that the young person we mentor is not fulfilling all our hopes and dreams for him or her. But we can be thankful for the difference that we have made in his or her life. We may support people as they go through personal struggles with addiction or depression, only to see them fall into despair again. We can take comfort in knowing that we were able to be faithful instruments of grace for them, if even for just a short time. Jesus healed the sick, but he did not totally obliterate all disease in his world. We are challenged to carry out our calling faithfully and to be thankful for that which we can accomplish for the sake of God and others. We still need the courage and conviction necessary to slay the dragons set in our path.

Sometimes the path of our faith journey takes us through places we would rather not go. At times we must go forth and face the unknown or look inward and face ourselves. We might know that we are heading for dark times, but we must persevere and keep hope until we make it through. This is the trail of trials. These trials call us to look inward and learn about ourselves and grow. But after important and difficult times of introspection, we still need to slay the dragons in our path. We need to learn to love our neighbor and to love ourselves in concrete ways. How do we find the strength necessary to slay the dragons in our path? The Christian faith offers a strange way. In the next chapter we will explore the way of Christ—which is a way of sacrifice.

Questions for Reflection

Which trial from the fantasy stories engaged you the most? What was it about the scene that moved you?

What unknown aspect of your life frightens you the most? Have you ever passed up an opportunity to help yourself or to serve God because you were afraid of the unknown?
What are you learning about yourself?

What are some areas of your life that you like to keep closed away and hidden, even from yourself?

How can your faith help you accept or redeem your relationship with your parents or children?

Have you ever had to forge your own way, a way that was different from that of your parents?

What are some of the difficult and dangerous times that you have had to travel through in your life? Have you emerged from them? What did you learn about yourself? How did these experiences change you? What role did your faith play in helping you through the difficulties?

Have you ever had to take a step forward to confront an evil and known that there was no turning back? What steps into the labyrinth might you be called on to take in the future?

What dragons do you feel called to slay? That is, how can you make a difference in the world today? What are the evil dragons in your community? How can your Church confront these dragons?

The Way of Christ: Images of Christ and Sacrifice

When my son, Nathan, was quite young, he and I watched the film *The Iron Giant.*The film is about a giant robot who falls to Earth from outer space. The robot wants nothing more than to be a hero like Superman. But he discovers that he was created to be a weapon and is in fact the most powerful weapon that the Earth has ever seen. Some of the adults on Earth discover this fact, and set out to destroy him with a bomb. However, the bomb also threatens the lives of innocent bystanders. When the attack comes, the robot must decide whether to fight back, run away, or sacrifice himself to save the humans. He chooses to take the full brunt of a bomb attack and is blown to pieces. My son was devastated. He was sad, he was angry, and he was crushed. But then, at the very end of the film, we saw the scattered pieces of the giant robot begin to move back together, and my son's sorrow turned to joy.

Tales of heroic sacrifice have been around for as long as stories have been told. These stories flow from humankind's recognition of a truth that may not seem rational yet somehow makes perfect sense: sacrifice can bring redemption. Christians know this story most profoundly in the Gospel story of Jesus Christ.

Images of Christ in Fiction and Film

"Christ figure" is a term that critics use to describe a character in fiction or film that demonstrates the characteristics of Jesus Christ. Many Christians are surprised to discover that it is quite common to find Christ figures in fiction and film. We might fail to recognize this Christ imagery, especially if the character in question is not a man who wears a beard and talks as we imagined Jesus of Nazareth talked.

In *E.T.: The Extra-Terrestrial,* the alien E.T. can be seen as a Christ figure. E.T. comes to our world as an innocent child. He has healing power and brings love and redemption to those around him. He is persecuted and crucified by the authorities of his time, dies, and then rises again. He tells his friends that he will be with them in their heads and hearts, and then ascends back home to the heavens, presumably to be with his heavenly parent. To say that E.T. is a Christ figure is not to say that his story parallels every single aspect of the life of Christ. E.T. is not presented as the perfect child of God, for example, and Jesus is not an alien from another planet who arrives by spaceship. The analogies are sure to break down at some point.

As a matter of fact, Christ-imagery can be most thought provoking when some aspects of the character are quite different from Jesus Christ. This technique—known as defamiliarization—can help us reflect on aspects of the Christ story in new ways. Jack Nicholson's character, McMurphy, in *One Flew Over the Cuckoo's Nest* is also a Christ figure, but is different from Jesus in many ways. This Oscar-winning R-rated film is quite disturbing, and is not intended for children. McMurphy is a patient in a mental hospital who says and does vulgar things that are not Christlike at all. But his efforts to resist the hospital staff, especially the controlling and oppressive Nurse Ratched, challenge the other inmates to strive for personal freedom and to stop passively accepting the rules on their floor. Viewing McMurphy as a Christ figure can shock us out of our familiarity with the Gospel story so that we can see Christ in a new way. The story challenges us to recognize that Jesus too was a nonconformist who defied the authorities of his day. He gathered people around him and urged them to be free and to challenge those in authority. Because of this, the authorities saw him as a danger to their power. They labeled him a crazy man, and they put him to death. Still, in the end his death brought redemption and freedom to those around him.

To say that characters such as E.T., McMurphy, or Harry Potter can serve as Christ figures is certainly not to say that we are putting them on a par with Jesus or that they should be objects of worship. It is merely to say that these characters share some aspects of Christ and offer us the opportunity to reflect on the Christ story from fresh perspectives.

Many Christians might be surprised to find that many authors and screenwriters include intentional allusions to the life of Christ in their films and novels. But not all Christ imagery is intentional. It is common for authors and filmmakers of a variety of faiths to tell stories in which a noble character sacrifices himself or herself for the sake of another. The author or screenwriter may not be aware of any parallels between their story and the Christ story; they may be simply expressing the deep truths that are bred in our bones. It is a story that resonates with us as humans. From the earliest of times, people have told stories of heroes who lay down their life for the sake of their friends. Through the eyes of faith, we can see these as expressions of the innermost longings of the heart of humankind and the recognition of a profound religious truth.

Images of Christ in Today's Fantasy Stories

Harry Potter, Luke Skywalker, and Frodo Baggins, as well as other characters in the stories, can be seen as Christ figures. Again, this is not to say that these characters are exactly like Jesus or as good as Jesus was. They all have flaws, and the analogies break down at some point. But each provides us with an opportunity to reflect on one or more aspects of the story of Christ.

Fawkes the Phoenix

In *Harry Potter and the Chamber of Secrets,* Harry meets Professor Dumbledore's pet phoenix, Fawkes. The phoenix is a birdlike creature found in Greek, Egyptian, Islamic, and European mythology. It sings a beautiful song, sheds healing tears, and bursts into flames, only to rise from the ashes to be born again. Fawkes fits this ancient pattern. Harry is shocked to see Fawkes burst into flames and die in Professor Dumbledore's office. But later Fawkes is reborn, and singing his beautiful song, he comes to Harry's aid and heals Harry's wounds with his tears.

Later, we learn that those who work to resist evil in their world call themselves the Order of the Phoenix.

Christians throughout the ages have seen the phoenix as a symbol of Christ. Artists have depicted Christ, like the phoenix, as the singer of a beautiful song.[1] Like the phoenix, we recognize Christ as the wounded healer who heals through personal pain and sorrow (1 Pet. 2:24). Of course the most obvious and dramatic analogy is the death and resurrection of the phoenix and of Christ. Miraculously, new life comes through pain and death.

Harry Potter

Harry Potter is known throughout the wizarding world as a savior. People know that even as a young baby, he saved the world from evil. Although he is magical, he enters into our own muggle world, a world that does not recognize him for who he really is. In the climactic scene of *Harry Potter and the Sorcerer's Stone,* Harry makes the decision to face evil. He subjects himself to great pain when he grabs onto the source of evil and refuses to let it go until he has stopped it. Harry is willing to die to save his world from the evil Voldemort. He loses consciousness at the end of the battle and lies in the hospital for three days before he rises again. Although there is much to celebrate, Harry knows that the threat of Voldemort and his evil is not over.

By reflecting on Harry's story, we are able to reflect on the courage of Christ's redemptive act: his entrance into our world as a baby, his conscious choice to follow the way of death, and the joy of his resurrection. We also recognize that, even after Christ's victory, the battle against evil goes on.

Lily Potter

When Harry Potter was just one year old, his mother, Lily, sacrificed herself, taking on herself the lethal curse of Voldemort in order to save Harry's life. Throughout the Harry Potter stories, we learn that this sacrificial act of love has long-lasting power. As Professor Dumbledore tells Harry:

> "Your mother died to save you. If there is one thing Voldemort cannot understand, it is love. He didn't realize that love as powerful as your mother's for you leaves its own mark. Not a scar, no visible sign. . . . To have been loved so deeply, even though the person who loved us is gone, will give us some protection forever."[2]

This sacrificial act of love—described as "strong magic"—saves Harry several times over.[3] Loving sacrifice has the power to redeem us and restore us. Christians know this redemptive love most profoundly through Christ's sacrifice for us.

The image of Lily Potter can help us reflect on the power of Christ's act of love. Harry is forever marked by his mother's love, and the Book of Ephesians says that through Christ Christians are "marked with the seal of the promised Holy Spirit" (1:13). Christ's love, like Lily's love for Harry, protects us and has eternal effects.

Obi-Wan Kenobi

Obi-Wan Kenobi is a wise teacher of spiritual truths who is misunderstood by those around him. He serves as a guide to his disciples, and in *Star Wars: A New Hope,* he sacrifices himself to save his friends.[4] As he tells Vader, "If you strike me down, I shall become more powerful than you can possibly imagine." After he suffers this physical death, he is able to always be with Luke on a spiritual plane.

We can use this image to reflect on the way Christ lay down his life for his friends, and how Christ is now able to be with them spiritually "always, to the end of the age" (Matt. 28:20).

Luke Skywalker

Return of the Jedi parallels the Christ story in its tale of sacrifice and redemption. Confronted with pain and the threat of death at the hands of the Emperor, Luke Skywalker refuses to use violence. Instead, he chooses the way of pain and the way of peace. At the end of the film, it is only by being willing to let go of his life that Luke forces Darth Vader's hand. The act redeems Vader and prompts him to take action, and he rids the galaxy of evil by ending the Sith Lord's reign of terror. Even though everyone else seems to dismiss Vader as pure evil with no chance for redemption, Luke insists that he senses the potential for good in him. After Vader's redemption, he suffers a fatal blow. Luke tells him, "I've got to save you." Vader's reply is, "You already have, Luke."

Only by the suffering of the son, Luke Skywalker, is Darth Vader, and ultimately the whole universe, saved. Vader sees the example of Luke's sacrificial act, and then sacrifices his own life for the sake of Luke and for the sake of what is right and good.

We can use this image to reflect on how Christ rejected the way of violence and chose the path of suffering as the way to victory. Jesus refused to use his power for violence and instead inspired many to strive for peace and to take a stand for what is right and good.

Anakin Skywalker

Anakin Skywalker is a different kind of Christ figure. His story spans the entire six films of the series. It is a story about his fall, his need for redemption, and how he ultimately becomes a redeemer himself. In *The Phantom Menace,* it is implied that his was a virgin birth. The word *Christ* literally means "the anointed one" or "the chosen one," and Anakin is referred to in the same way. Ultimately, Anakin sacrifices himself to save the universe from the power of evil. And at the end of *Return of the Jedi,* Anakin appears to Luke, along with Yoda and Obi-Wan Kenobi, in a transfigured way.

We can use this image to reflect on the nature of salvation and of the Savior. How is it the same as the Christ story? How is it different? Anakin Skywalker was prophesied to "bring balance to the Force." Did Christ bring the spiritual nature of the universe into balance, tip the balance in favor of good, or totally defeat evil?

Frodo Baggins

In *The Lord of the Rings,* Frodo Baggins's story parallels Christ's story in several ways. Frodo's redemptive act is one of letting go of power. He does not embrace the power of the Ring as something to wield for his own sake, but instead he attempts to destroy it.

Frodo is wounded by the knife of a Black Rider on Weathertop, a symbol of the supernatural power of evil. He lays unconscious for three days while Elrond tends to him. He is able to rise up, but Elrond warns Frodo that he will always carry his wound with him.

We can use the image of Frodo to reflect on how Christ, who had great power, "did not regard equality with God as something to be exploited, but emptied himself . . . and became obedient to the point of death—even death on a cross" (Phil. 2:6–8). In so doing he received wounds that Thomas could see even in his resurrected form (John 20:24–29). Frodo's struggle with his burden can help us reflect on how Jesus willingly chose the path to the cross, and the loneliness and sorrow of the journey.

Arwen Evenstar

In the film *The Lord of the Rings: The Fellowship of the Ring,* Arwen Evenstar is depicted as even more of a Christ figure than she is in the novel. Arwen is an elf who gives up her immortality to marry Aragorn, a mortal man. She takes on human mortality for the sake of love. In the film version, she saves Frodo and prays: "What grace is given me, let it pass to him. Let him be spared. Save him."

Using this image, we can reflect on the incarnation of Jesus Christ: how he took on human flesh for the sake of love, and how he gave of his grace to save us.

Aragorn

In *The Lord of the Rings,* the scruffy northern ranger known as Strider does not appear to be royalty. Yet we come to recognize that Strider, also known as Aragorn, son of Arathorn, is the long-awaited King of Gondor, whom the prophets said would return in the time of need to conquer evil. As Ioreth, wise woman of Gondor said, "The hands of the king are the hands of a healer, and thus shall the rightful king be known."[5] Aragorn indeed heals the sick and demonstrates courage, character, and nobility in accepting his call to be king.

We can use this imagery to reflect on the way people yearned for Christ's coming for centuries, and how Jesus, the descendent of King David, fulfilled the age-old prophecies. We can also reflect on the way Jesus was not recognized by the world as the messiah. In the Gospel of Mark, the crowd around the cross mockingly calls Jesus a healer and a king (15:18, 32). But those of us who believe the message of the Gospels recognize that their words are true. Jesus is indeed the great healer and the great king.

Gandalf

Gandalf is a worker of wonders, a wise guide, and a teacher of truths. As he enters the Mines of Moria, readers sense that he suspects he is going to his personal doom. He does not want to take that path if he can avoid it, but he does so because he must. Facing the Balrog in the Mines of Moria, Gandalf sacrifices himself to save his friends. In the film version of *The Lord of the Rings: The Fellowship of the Ring,* the Christ-figure motif is given a visual nod. As Gandalf falls into the abyss, his arms are wide open in cruciform, echoing the posture of Christ on the cross. In *The Two Towers,* when Gandalf returns on horseback, he is now Gandalf the White, the White Rider. Aragorn, Gimli, and Legolas do not recognize him at first in his resurrected form, but rejoice when they realize that their friend has returned.

We can use this image of Christ to reflect on Jesus as a leader and a powerful worker of wonders. Though he would have gladly taken another path, he followed the path God had laid out for him, and sacrificed himself to save others. The comparison can also be made to Christ's resurrection. The Book of Revelation uses the image of Christ as a rider on a white horse (19:11). And like Gandalf's companions, Jesus' disciples initially failed to recognize him in his resurrected form (John 20:11–18, 21:1–14) much as we may fail to recognize Christ when Christ appears to us today (Matt. 25:31–46).

Smaller Sacrifices

Many of the previous examples not only provide us with images of Jesus Christ, but on a more basic level, function within the context of their stories to demonstrate the nobility of characters and to illustrate the practical effectiveness of personal sacrifice. This is a profound truth. In the Christ story, God wrote a story in which sacrifice had the power to save the world. But such power also exists on a smaller scale.

In today's fantasy stories, we find many examples of smaller sacrifices that call the characters—and by extension, us—to give up comfort or safety for a greater cause. In *Harry Potter and the Sorcerer's Stone,* Ron Weasley makes just this kind of sacrifice. Near the climax of the story, Ron, Harry, and Hermione become living game pieces in a life-sized match of wizard's chess. This is frightening because in wizard's chess, game pieces violently attack each other when they take another piece. In what was perhaps the most intense scene in the film, Ron sacrifices himself, allowing himself to be attacked in order to help his friends move forward in their quest. It is important to note that Ron does not make his sacrifice under pressure from others. Harry and Hermione do not bully Ron or manipulate him into doing this. As a matter of fact, they try to talk him out of making the move. But Ron selflessly moves into the strategic square and allows himself to be attacked and his piece taken.

Ron's selfless act illustrates the principle that sometimes we need to make personal sacrifices to further the cause of good. The Apostle Paul presented sacrifice as a way of life for Christians. He wrote, "I appeal to you therefore, brothers and sisters, by the mercies of God, to present your bodies as a living sacrifice, holy and acceptable to God, which is your spiritual worship" (Rom. 12:1).

Another smaller sacrifice we are sometimes called to make is letting go of past grudges and complaints in order to heal a friendship or a marriage. In *Harry Potter and the Prisoner of Azkaban,* Ron and Hermione are not speaking to each other because of a disagreement about their pets. Eventually they realize that they need to let go of their grudge and to heal their friendship to help protect Harry from the threat of Sirius Black.

Relationships are often redeemed when we are willing to let go of our anger. We can never really win an argument with a friend or a spouse, but we can find reconciliation. Although we should not deny our problems, we need to find a way to let go of past complaints in order to move ahead in our relationships (1 Cor. 13:5–6). When I was serving as a pastor, a number of troubled couples came to me, wanting me to judge who was right and who was wrong. I would tell them that when it comes to relationships, it is not about who is right and who is wrong; it is about finding a way to get along. Instead of finding a way to win an argument, we need to find a way for both parties to win.

Sometimes the only way we can succeed in our life's mission is by making the smaller sacrifice of giving up power or other opportunities. At the end of *The Empire Strikes Back,* Luke Skywalker is face-to-face with Darth Vader, and in mortal danger as he hangs on the edge of a tunnel that leads into the empty abyss of space. He is offered a choice between joining Vader to rule the galaxy and suffering a painful death. In a close-up shot, Luke is seen looking to Vader and then to the vast abyss below him. He makes his decision and lets go, falling into the abyss—presumably to his doom—rather than joining the Dark Side. By letting go, Luke saves his soul.

Like Luke Skywalker, we can see that it is not only by winning battles that we achieve victory; often it is by letting go. Sometimes the victory is won by sacrificing opportunities for money, power, or fame in order to follow a path of service and integrity. This may mean taking a job that is less glamorous, but allows us to serve others while staying true to our calling. It may mean that we refuse to act immorally at work, even though it means we may lose a potential raise, promotion, or even our job. We may need to let go of an unhealthy relationship for the sake of our spiritual life, even though that relationship makes us feel good in the moment. In the Gospel of Matthew, Jesus says, "For what will it profit them if they gain the whole world but forfeit their life?" (16:26). There are times when we are called to let go of these opportunities for the sake of our soul.

Sometimes the sacrifice that we are asked to make is not small at all. We may be asked to give up our way of life, or even our life itself, for the sake of what God is calling us to do. In *The Lord of the Rings,* Frodo Baggins and Samwise Gamgee model two types of sacrifice. Frodo is faced with a difficult decision when he is asked to give up his comfortable life to spearhead a vital quest. He knows that it is going to be difficult and will even place his life in danger. But Frodo is willing to make that sacrifice. Though this may seem to be the stuff of fantasy, in our times people such as Martin Luther King Jr., Archbishop Oscar Romero of El Salvador, and the Mahatma Gandhi have followed Jesus' teachings and taken on a cause that they knew would likely lead to their own deaths.

Samwise Gamgee risked his life for the sake of the quest, but he also serves as an excellent model of someone who makes smaller daily sacrifices. Practically every day of the quest, he makes small sacrifices. He gives up some of his sleep time to stay awake on watch duty so Frodo can get more sleep. He gives up some of his share of the food so Frodo will have more to eat. By putting Frodo's well-being in front of his own, Sam is helping their cause and demonstrating selfless love. These small, almost unnoticeable sacrifices are the type of daily sacrifices we are called to make. Our weekly tithes and offerings to our churches and our donations to charity are regular acts of sacrifice for a higher cause, as is giving our time to do important work in our church and in our community.

For Christians, Jesus serves as the ultimate example of someone who was willing to lay down his life for his friends. It is important to note that Christians do not understand this act to be one of powerlessness, but of power. Jesus did not become anyone's doormat. He was not a masochist. He did not passively sit back and let other people determine the agenda for his life. Jesus made a conscious choice of self-sacrifice, as do the heroes of today's fantasy stories, because he saw the higher purpose that would be served by it.

The call to sacrifice is not a call to a dysfunctional, codependent relationship with others. We are not expected to let ourselves be abused or dominated. But at times we are called to give up some of our wants, desires, or possessions for the sake of others. Our personal sacrifices may not save the whole world, but they can help others and help God's cause. What is more, our sacrifices often serve as our own salvation as well.

We face many challenges on our journey. These challenges can lead us to hang on tightly to whatever we have or to cling to our desires for the future. But sometimes our path out of trouble follows the way of Christ. By sacrificing ourselves in big and small ways, we are able to move forward in our faith journey.

Questions for Reflection

Which Christ-figure from the fantasy stories is the most helpful for you? Why?

Which Christ-figure from the fantasy stories was least helpful for you? Why?

What other Christ figures have you seen in popular fiction or films?

Do you have a relationship that is harmed because you are hanging onto a grudge or your pride? How can you give these up in order to save the relationship?

Do you have legitimate concerns about the health of one of your relationships? Does someone else pressure you to give up more of yourself than what is healthy?

God does not call us to abusive codependant relationships. Does your desire to be a sacrificial person ever put you in danger of being abused in your relationships? In what ways are such relationships unhealthy and not glorifying God?

What might you need to sacrifice or give up for the greater good?

What daily or weekly sacrifices have you been called to make?

There and Back Again: Celebrating and Returning from the Journey

At the end of my last year of college, the campus ministry group to which I belonged had a big party to celebrate all that God had done for us and all that had been accomplished in our ministry. God had touched many of our lives, and our campus group had grown considerably that year. We had a great deal to celebrate.

During the party I asked a friend of mine if she was looking forward to her summer break. She answered, "Yes and no." She explained that at the beginning of the school year, she had made a real commitment to Jesus Christ for the first time. But she had not realized how much that commitment had changed her until she went home for spring break. While she was home, she met her old high school friends and realized that she no longer shared their goals or values. And though she still had fun hanging around with them, she decided not to join them for some of their more questionable activities. She and her friends no longer shared the bond they once did.

Meanwhile, all her mother wanted to talk about was the new furniture she had purchased after years of wanting it. Admiring her living room set, her mother said, "I've finally achieved my life's goal." My friend realized that her goals were now quite different from those of her family. Going home made my friend realized that she was no longer the same person who had left home the previous fall. She felt some sadness in this realization. Her relationships with her friends and family had changed, and she sensed their confusion and suspicion over the changes they saw in her. At the same time, she was pleased to realize how far she had come in her faith journey.

Celebrations

Harry Potter's first three years at Hogwarts each end with joyous celebratory feasts. They have plenty of food, and individuals and groups of people receive recognition for their accomplishments. As we read the books, these celebrations do not strike the reader as inappropriate. Instead, they are presented as fitting expressions of pleasure and appreciation for what has happened during the year. Harry and his friends suspect that the evil Voldemort will rise again, but that does not stop them from celebrating what has been accomplished. They need this time of celebration, and in a way, we as readers need it as well.

Celebrations are a recurring motif in the *Star Wars* films as well. *The Phantom Menace* ends with a grand parade celebrating the victory of the planet Naboo. The end of *Star Wars: A New Hope* features a formal celebration and public recognition of the accomplishments of Luke Skywalker and his friends. The Empire has not been destroyed, but they still have cause to celebrate. The end of *Return of the Jedi,* which serves as the ending for the entire series of six *Star Wars* films, features a celebration on the grandest of scales. A few brief shots in *Return of the Jedi: Special Edition* (1997) reveal that the entire galaxy, from Cloud City to Tatooine to Coruscant, is celebrating the victory over the Empire.

The Lord of the Rings trilogy opens with Bilbo Baggins's long expected eleventy-first birthday party. Hobbits' knack for throwing parties and their capacity to enjoy them are presented as virtues in the books. Hobbits really know how to have a good time with family and friends! Bilbo's party features plenty of food and drink, speeches, and even fireworks. The trilogy culminates with a grand royal wedding and a coronation. Although these events are more subdued than

Bilbo's party, they are still clearly joyful gatherings. Aragorn's love and thanksgiving are evident in his words and in his care to acknowledge all who had helped him in his quest. It becomes evident that humans and elves know how to hold grand liturgies to mark significant moments in their history.

Many people think of parties and religion as being at the opposite ends of human experience. Can we party—*really* party—to celebrate the goodness of God? The Bible suggests that it is not only possible but desirable. The nation of Israel was commanded to set aside times of the year for national and religious celebrations, or feasts. These were not just wild, anything-goes parties, but neither were they solemn religious rituals. They were joyful celebrations of thanksgiving to God, featuring music, song, dance, a lot of food, and worship. So, although the ultimate purpose of these feasts was to praise God, people were expected to enjoy themselves in the process. As the Book of Ecclesiastes puts it, there is "a time to weep, and a time to laugh; a time to mourn, and a time to dance" (3:4).

The Gospels tell us that Jesus described the Reign of God as a feast (Luke 14:15–24) and as a wedding (Matt. 22:1–10). Jesus himself attended a wedding feast, and performed his first miracle there by turning water into wine (John 2:1–11). Jesus did not take the ascetic approach to life that John the Baptist did, and he knew that some religious people would criticize him because of it. He characterized people's reaction to him by saying, "The Son of Man came eating and drinking, and they say, 'Look, a glutton and a drunkard, a friend to tax collectors and sinners!'" (Matt. 11:19).

Christians have cause to celebrate. We have an awesome God who loves us and has given us life. God gives us a wondrous world, has called us to an amazing adventure, has provided us with all the provisions we need for our journey, has given us traveling companions, and gives us hope to make it through the rough times. So, why is it that we can feel so awkward about celebrating? Somehow, in our Western culture at least, celebrating does not seem very religious. The Psalmist calls for praise of God that includes a variety of instruments, including percussion, and even dancing (Ps. 150), but some of our weekly worship resembles a solemn funeral more than a joyous celebration.

Yet, we have the opportunity to get together with people in our faith communities to celebrate the joy of God's good creation and the life God gives us. These celebrations can take us beyond the fun of conventional parties and into rich expressions of joy that come from knowing God and God's people. When our churches are able to launch a new mission in the community or experience growth in an existing ministry, we should celebrate and thank God for everything God has done. We can acknowledge those who have served God well, and celebrate God's work in our midst. Our celebrations can be offered as worship to God, and we can enjoy ourselves in the process.

In Haiti many people face struggles every day to earn a living. But when it is time for a wedding, the Christian communities rally together to make it an extravagant and joyful celebration. They give tribute to the living God by acknowledging the joy of living. This does not mean that they abandon the responsibility of making ends meet or cease striving for economic justice. But it does mean that they recognize the importance of marking important times and using those celebrations as a way of expressing their joy and thanksgiving to God.

Our faith journey is enriched when we celebrate the important times of our life and the life of our faith community. We can do this in our churches or in our homes with our friends and family. As we celebrate, we give thanks to God and express the joy of living the life God has given us. And we can feel free to enjoy ourselves in the process. Sometimes, it seems, we need to take a cue from Luke Skywalker, and take time to party with the Ewoks!

Home from the journey

One of the important steps of the hero's journey in ancient myths is her or his return home. Often the hero returns home to face harsh realities. After such exciting and epic successes, Harry Potter must return each year to his muggle home on Privet Drive, with the Dursleys. At Hogwarts Harry has friends, he is recognized as the best Quidditch player at school, and he is admired for his heroic acts. None of this is acknowledged on Privet Drive. At the end of *Harry Potter and the Sorcerer's Stone,* Harry realizes that in many ways, Hogwarts is now his real home. But returning to his childhood home on Privet Drive gives him perspective, keeps him humble, and as we learn in *Harry Potter and the Order of the Phoenix,* offers Harry protection as well.

In the *Star Wars* films, the return home is a time of trial and a time for the hero to realize how much he has changed. In *Return of the Jedi,* Luke Skywalker must return to Tatooine to rescue his friend from Jabba the Hut. The opening shots of his face reveal that Luke is not the same fresh-faced boy who left Tatooine years earlier. He is now a Jedi, and ready to take on danger. Luke takes on the responsibility of confronting trouble on his home planet. In *The Attack of the Clones,* Anakin Skywalker's return home to Tatooine is also a trial, but Anakin does not fare as well in his test as his son would later. He had neither stayed connected to his roots nor kept in contact with his mother. Thus, when he faces the crisis of losing her, he is unable to integrate his life off-world with his roots on Tatooine. As a result he takes a further step toward evil and power.

In *The Return of the King,* Frodo, Sam, Merry, and Pippin must return to Hobbiton after their adventures in faraway lands. There they find that the mysterious Sharky and his ruffians have taken over their hometown, destroying the land and oppressing its residents. But these hobbits do not accept the situation with a shrug and the thought that one can never go home. Their journeys have empowered them. They now know—better than ever—who they are, what they stand for, and what they are capable of doing. They rise up against the oppressor and throw him out of town.

According to the Gospel of Luke, after his baptism, calling, temptation in the desert, and successful beginning of his teaching ministry, Jesus had an eventful return to his hometown of Nazareth (Luke 4:16–30). Jesus is not the same person he was as a child or young man. The Gospel tells us that when he returned, he entered the synagogue, read from the scroll of the prophet Isaiah, and boldly proclaimed his identity as the promised one of God, who would bring freedom, healing, and justice to the people. This was not a welcome message. The people of Nazareth are taken aback and say, "Is not this Joseph's son?" (Luke 4:22). Jesus responds by saying, "Truly I tell you, no prophet is accepted in the prophet's hometown" (Luke 4:24).

We can use these stories of homecoming to reflect on our faith journey in two ways. First, we can reflect on those times when we literally come home after being away for a period of time. As we go forth on our faith journey, we grow and change. We may come to be respected and admired by others at work, at school, or in the town or city in which we now live. But back home we may be received as the same old kid who grew up there. This can be frustrating. At times like this, it may be helpful to remember that even Jesus was not given a hero's welcome when he returned to his hometown, nor, it seems, did he expect it. Still, while he was at home, he stayed true to who he was, and did not try to deny it.

Some Christians come to embrace their faith journey only after leaving home. Some, like my friend from college, may find that their family or friends do not believe that they have really turned their life around or do not understand their newfound faith. It can be disheartening to recognize that we have changed and grown apart from those with whom we grew up. But it can also be helpful for us to touch base with those who knew us when we were young, and to reflect on how far God has taken us.

A second way to reflect on returning home is on a more symbolic level. We never truly come home from our faith journey. It lasts our whole life long. But we may well have to come back to earth after a mountaintop experience in our spiritual life—an experience of feeling especially close to God and having a strong desire to live out God's will for our life. These times—often found during retreats, conferences, or meaningful experiences in our local congregations—are a real blessing and an important step in our faith journey. But we are not called to reach a highly spiritual state of mind and neglect the needs of life around us. Like Merry, Pippin, Sam, and Frodo, we come back home changed and empowered to make a difference in our own surroundings.

Some Christians can fall into the trap of living in a sort of Christian subculture or fantasy land. They travel from their church to the Christian bookstore, riding in their cars listening to Christian radio stations, and then back home, where they are surrounded by Christian art and books and only have contact with Christian friends. They attempt to insulate themselves from the outside world. But if we are to be the salt and light of the world, then we must live in the wider world God has given us. We must engage our culture and the people in that culture. This can be tough. Sometimes we would like to be able to stay on the mountaintop and ignore the messy problems below. But we have not been called to live our lives in the heavens. Instead, we are called to live on earth, to get to know the people and their needs, and to minister to them.

In the past century, perhaps no literary "common person" has gone on as epic a journey as Samwise Gamgee. Sam had never left the Shire before, but his journey takes him to extraordinary places, and he sees many amazing things. In the process he experiences great personal growth and, at the same time, accomplishes great good for the world. One suspects that his epic experiences of facing Shelob, the giant spider, and murderous orcs in faraway lands give Sam the courage to carry out the no-less-epic task of asking Rosie to marry him. He has had a great adventure, and knows just how wondrous his world is and how wondrous he is. But he also knows where he belongs. He has come to know his place in the world. It is fitting, then, that the story ends with Sam returning home to his wife and child, drawing a deep breath, and saying, "Well, I'm back."[1]

As we come to the end of this faith journey through the fantasy lands, let us give thanks for the insights that God has given us. May we celebrate God's goodness, recognize how we have been changed by our journey, and bring our newfound strength and courage back home to minister for God in our world.

Questions for Reflection

What do you have to celebrate with your faith community? What do you and your friends have to celebrate? What do you and your family have to celebrate?

Have you ever experienced worship as real celebration? What aspects of worship are celebratory for you? How can you help your congregational worship be more celebratory?

Have you been to parties that were not held at a church, but that turned out to be a positive *spiritual* experience? What made them positive spiritual experiences? How might you host such a party or gathering?

Are you ever tempted to disengage from the world around you?

Can you think of a time that you had a "mountaintop" experience? Did you have a hard time going back home? What made it difficult?

How do you live out the charge to live in the world but not be of the world?

What opportunities for spiritual reflection did you find in these fantasy stories that were not covered in the chapters of this book?

Dangers along the Path: Cautions and Concerns

This section is different from the chapters that have come before it. While the previous chapters explored spiritual themes in the fantasy stories, this section of the book steps outside the stories to address some of the questions that have been raised about them. Many of these questions deal with the Harry Potter stories in particular, while others apply to all the fantasy stories, and to many other stories of our popular culture as well. Some questions are raised by parents or others who may not have read the books or watched the films but who are worried about what they have heard. In other cases, people who have read the stories and watched the films have identified some concerns. They enjoy the stories and recognize some of the positive themes in them, but do not know what to think about some of the controversies in the Christian community surrounding these stories. This section raises some of these issues and offers some reflections on them.

Putting the Controversy into Context

Before addressing some of the particular concerns raised about these stories, it is important to put the controversies into perspective. Some articles and television news stories give the impression that all Christians are unanimously opposed to Harry Potter and other fantasy stories. This is simply not true. Some media outlets try to grab our attention by highlighting controversies and extreme opinions. A number of articles and news stories have done this by first quoting an "unreasonable Christian" who opposes the books, and then interviewing a "reasonable person on the street," who thinks that the stories are harmless. Such articles and news stories perpetuate the stereotype that Christians are frightened about and negative toward everything in the wider world. Christians may see these reports and feel that in order to be a loyal Christian, they should oppose these stories altogether. Indeed, many Christians have voiced concerns about these stories, but many Christian voices, including conservative Christian voices, are expressing the view that these stories are harmless and even helpful.

The evangelical Protestant magazine *Christianity Today* praised the Harry Potter stories in both an editorial and a film review.[1] Conservative Christian commentator Chuck Colson has said that the Harry Potter stories "inspire the imagination within a Christian framework—and prepare the hearts of readers for the real-life story of Christ."[2] The *Star Wars* films have their fair share of Christian fans, and they have even inspired a *Star Wars* Christian fan Web site.[3] Likewise, many Catholic and conservative Protestant groups have praised the spiritual messages in *The Lord of the Rings*.[4]

Differences of opinion have led to tensions within churches and even between Christian friends. It is important to recognize that wise people of good will can disagree with one another. In *The Fellowship of the Ring,* Gandalf and Aragorn disagree over the best path to take to the other side of the mountains. Within the Christian community, the Apostles Paul and Peter disagreed over issues such as table fellowship with Gentiles. We must acknowledge that there is more than one Christian perspective on each of these stories. Some Christians want nothing to do with Harry Potter, or even a book like the one you are reading now. But no matter what our views are, it is important that we do not become arrogant in our attitudes toward those who disagree with us. We should not disrespect others, nor should we allow them to disrespect us or discount our faith. Our opinions about the issues that follow should not become barriers to our fellowship with one another. Hopefully these differences of opinion can even prompt some helpful dialogue.

Concerns with Witchcraft and Wizardry

Perhaps the single most divisive issue surrounding today's fantasy stories is the use of witchcraft and wizardry in them. The discussion that follows first provides background on sorcery, the occult, and Wicca. Next, it explains why it is difficult to make the case that these fantasy stories are explicitly promoting the modern practice of witchcraft. Finally, it examines reasons why parents, teachers, and others might still be concerned about the presence of sorcery in these stories.

Several passages in the Bible condemn the practice of magic, witchcraft, and sorcery, which is the use of supernatural powers through the assistance of spirits. In the Old Testament, the people of Israel were commanded to drive out sorcerers, soothsayers, those who practiced divination, and those who cast spells, because such things are abhorrent to the Lord (Deut. 18: 9–12, Exod. 22:18). In the New Testament, the Apostle Paul lists sorcery as a vice, right alongside immorality, licentiousness, and idolatry (Gal. 5:19–21).

Today a variety of occult groups and Wicca covens practice forms of sorcery and witchcraft. The occult is a general term for the belief in and performance of magic, divination, and other secretive and supernatural practices. Wicca is a neopagan belief system that promotes the practice of witchcraft. Some people have confused Wicca with Satanism, which is the overt worship of the devil. To be clear on the point, Wiccans do not believe in Satan, but then again they do not believe in a single all-powerful God either. Perhaps because Wicca groups promote feminist ideals and advocate for being in tune with nature, they have become increasingly successful at recruiting teenage girls. But Wicca is not a benign mainline religion, as it often tries to present itself to the public. Most Christians would be quite troubled by common Wiccan practices such as casting spells, working naked, and using ritual knives, and would be suspicious of the secretive nature of certain spells and practices that are made known only to members of a coven. Christians should know and should let others know that the occult and Wicca are theologically and philosophically inconsistent with Christianity. A person cannot consistently claim to be both a Wiccan and a Christian, and Christians should avoid any involvement with such groups.

The Harry Potter stories in particular have been the focus of a great deal of attention, as the children in the stories are learning to be wizards and witches. Harry and his friends attend Hogwarts School of Wizardry and Witchcraft, where they fly on broomsticks and learn to cast spells. Do the Harry Potter stories encourage the modern practice of witchcraft? There are several reasons why it is difficult to claim that they do. First of all, the author, J. K. Rowling, adamantly denies that this is her goal, and there is good reason to believe her. Rowling has been the victim of slanderous and completely unfounded rumors (often passed on by Christians) that accuse her of being a practicing witch who is using her books to recruit children into the occult and Wicca. Rowling does not talk much about her religious life, but she does make it clear that she is not a Wiccan but a Christian, that she attends a Christian church, and that she believes in God and not in magic.[5] She has also said that she has not met one child who became interested in becoming a witch because of her novels.[6]

Second, the magic performed in the Harry Potter stories does not serve as a beginners' guide to modern-day witchcraft, because the magic performed in them does not resemble the magic performed by occult groups. Students at Hogwarts learn to perform spells by learning to pronounce Latin or Latin-inspired words and twirling their wands in a certain way. The magic at Hogwarts is not presented as a religious practice that taps into the power of spirits. Many people who take the practice of witchcraft seriously have complained about this fact. They point out that, from the perspective of their serious beliefs in such matters, the books contain many errors.

Third, the books treat the magic that is performed in them as part of a world of make-believe. They draw on myths, legends, and popular fictional conventions of witchcraft and wizardry, and treat them as part of a fanciful world that includes flying cars, magical candy, dragons, griffons, unicorns, and centaurs. At one time people worried about having children watch *The Wizard of Oz* (1939) because it included both a good witch and a bad witch. They feared that this would prompt children to try to join occult groups to become good witches. When C. S. Lewis's Chronicles of Narnia was first released, they were criticized because they featured creatures from pagan mythology, heroes casting spells, witches doing magic, good characters reading the stars, and people using crystals.[7] Now these books are almost universally hailed in Christian circles. Over the years many Christian parents have observed that their children are able to distinguish between such fantasy worlds and reality, and therefore do not see these stories as a threat.

It is a hard stretch, then, to claim that these books are encouraging children to join Wicca, satanic, or other occult groups. Still, there are reasons to be concerned about sorcery and magic. The very fact that the Harry Potter books do not treat magic or witchcraft seriously is a concern to some. They see the threat of witchcraft as a serious one that should not be trivialized. They are troubled when people want to dismiss Christian protests of Harry Potter and the dangers of sorcery and witchcraft as laughable.[8] Those who hold Harry Potter book burnings and other such protests do not help in this regard. These protests can prompt people to dismiss Christians as extremists, and can lead them to defend not only the books but also occult groups themselves as harmless pastimes.

In addition, some of the official and unofficial tie-ins and cross-marketing merchandise available are of more concern than the books themselves. There is a troubling Lord of the Rings Oracle set, with "cards, map, and ring for divination and revelation," and Lord of the Rings Tarot Cards. One can only imagine how Professor Tolkien, a devout Christian, would have reacted to these. And although the Harry Potter books themselves may not prompt children to experiment with the occult, they have inspired some opportunistic marketers to release a number of "how to be a wizard" books and to hold events that encourage children to practice chanting spells.

Another concern is that while some people in Wicca and occult groups complain about what they see as inaccurate portrayals or trivialization of witchcraft in today's fantasy stories, others may be only too happy to use the books as recruiting tools, by making their practices sound as innocent and benign as those in the Harry Potter stories or as exciting and virtuous as those in *The Lord of the Rings*.

Without proper guidance, some of today's Christian fiction in which the heroes face demons and other powers of darkness can lead to an unhealthy interest in the occult. Some people have even become interested in satanic practices and the occult by reading the Bible. Because of this, it is important for Christians to talk about these issues with their children, students, and friends, no matter what books they are reading. We should warn others about the dangers of becoming involved with these groups, even the ones that seem to them to be harmless and cool at first glance.[9]

To say that the Harry Potter books, *Star Wars* films, and *The Lord of the Rings* do not explicitly promote Wicca is not to say that no other books or videos do so. We should be aware of what our children, students, and friends are watching. The recent video release *Scooby Doo and the Witch's Ghost* (1999), for example, plays like a primer and recruitment video for Wicca, offering several positive descriptions of the group and showing young cool Wiccans as part of a female rock band who overcome the discrimination they face to help Scooby and his friends save the day.

What is the answer? Should we attempt to shield our children and even other adults from such books? Every person of faith will need to come to his or her own decision on the matter. But today's fantasy stories do seem to provide us with an opportunity to do what we should be doing anyway, which is to talk to children about what they are reading and watching. We should let them know of other belief systems that out there, and that they will need to practice discernment in whatever they read or watch. When I was a child, my Christian parents allowed me to read many fantasy stories that featured wizards and sorcery, and even picture books of witches flying on broomsticks. But unlike those who raised children in my parents' generation, many of today's parents have genuine concerns that their children will have classmates who will invite them to join occult groups, Wicca, or satanic cults. Though the vast majority of fantasy lovers never enter these groups, parents will want to talk about this issue with their children.

Although we should warn people about the dangers of joining a cultlike group (including some cultlike churches), it can be harmful to spend too much time on such dark matters. We must guard against letting matters of the occult become an obsession or a cause for paranoia. Some Christians have lost their way by focusing on concerns about evil rather than the things of God. As Paul wrote to the church at Philippi, "Finally, beloved, whatever is true, whatever is honorable, whatever is just, whatever is pure, whatever is pleasing, whatever is commendable, if there is any excellence and if there is anything worthy of praise, think about these things" (Phil. 4:8).

Concerns about Questionable Virtues

Although the Harry Potter stories have been applauded by many Christians for the virtues they lift up,[10] other behaviors that the children model have given Christians pause. In the books, Harry, Ron, and Hermione lie to get out of trouble, break a host of school rules, demonstrate disrespect to adults who have authority over them, and take distinct pleasure in the misfortune of people they do not like, such as Draco Malfoy. Though these behaviors may be understandable and somewhat realistic for children, they are behaviors that many Christians frown on.

Ron Weasley represents an everyman in the Harry Potter stories, and his reactions are telling. In *Harry Potter and the Sorcerer's Stone,* when Hermione lies to the professors about an incident with a troll in the girls' bathroom, it raises her esteem in Ron's eyes. *In Harry Potter and the Chamber of Secrets,* when Professor McGonagall catches Harry and Ron sneaking around the castle, Harry concocts a lie to keep them out of trouble. Ron responds by telling Harry with admiration that it "was the best story you've ever come up with."[11] Later in that story, when Ron and Harry force an ill-prepared Gilderoy Lockhart to accompany them on their dangerous quest, they are certainly not being merciful and forgiving. In *Harry Potter and the Goblet of Fire,* when Harry and Ron's nemesis, Draco Malfoy, is turned into a ferret and bounced on the floor, Ron calls it "the best moment of my life."[12] Ron's reactions are understandable and very human. But it is important to realize that although Ron is a likeable character, he does not always function as a model of Christian virtue. He often says and does the things that we might want to say or do in a similar situation, but Harry and Hermione talk reason to him and try to get him to do what he *should* do.

Harry and Hermione have their own moments of rule-breaking, which are presented as harmless fun or as doing what must be done. Even Professor Dumbledore seems to admire the fact that Harry has "a certain disregard for rules."[13] This rule-breaking motif is played down somewhat in the film versions of the first two novels in the series, but it is still present.

How should Christians react to these behaviors? Some might defend the actions of Harry and his friends by pointing out that, according to the Gospels, Jesus himself broke many of the rules imposed on him in his day. He allowed his disciples to glean grain on the Sabbath (Matt. 12:1–8), and he healed people on the Sabbath as well (Mark 3:1–6), a practice commonly considered to be against Jewish law. He did not show great respect for the religious authorities. There is more than a bit of the rebel in Jesus' character. Of course, we must acknowledge that Jesus' case was different. Christians believe that Jesus was the Christ, and in truth had no higher human authority above him. Meanwhile, Harry, Ron, and Hermione are students at a school with teachers and a headmaster. Also, Jesus broke laws to accomplish greater good. Though Harry, Ron, and Hermione may think that they are breaking rules for the greater good, one suspects that they would have prevented a great deal of trouble if they had simply told Professors Dumbledore and McGonagall everything they knew as soon as they knew it. Had Harry, Ron, and Hermione done these things, it would have made them better models of virtue. However, it also would have made the stories much less exciting. Sometimes fictional characters do unreasonable things for the sake of drama.

On the other hand, as discussed in chapter 7, Harry, Ron, and Hermione model many virtues that we want our children to follow, such as mercy, courage, loyalty, and tolerance. How, then, should we respond? Are these stories teaching our children helpful or harmful behaviors? As stated earlier, no literary character should become a normative model of behavior for anyone. The answer lies in talking through these stories with our children, students, and friends, and teaching them to question and evaluate the fiction they watch and read.

Sometimes the concern is not with children modeling the questionable behaviors of the heroes of the stories, but with modeling the style and attitude of the villains. Dark characters can be found in any movie or book in which the forces of good battle against the forces of evil. For some teenagers in search of an edgy identity, the dress and manner of Darth Vader, Darth Maul, or the residents of Slytherin House are more appealing than that of the heroes. Occasional play-acting and experimenting with such roles can be normal and healthy, but a long-term obsession with things dark and grim is not healthy for children of any age.

Too Frightening for Children?

Today's fantasy stories feature many scenes that are violent and frightening to children. Should children read them or watch them? Some have raised this same concern regarding popular Bible stories that are read to children. Noah and his family survive the flood, but many drown. Young David is confronted by a giant and ends up killing him and cutting off his head. Jesus is tortured and crucified on the cross. Are these stories appropriate for children?

The original versions of many popular fairy tales are quite gruesome by today's standards. They depict children facing violent and frightening situations. In his book *The Uses of Enchantment: The Meaning and Importance of Fairy Tales,* Bruno Bettelheim argues that parents should not shield their children from these frightening fairy tales. According to Bettelheim, children know that the world can be a harsh and frightening place. He argues that they need to hear stories where people their own age overcome real danger in order to let them know that children can face awful situations and still find a happy ending.[14] By watching and telling scary stories, children can work through their fears and be better prepared to face the world.

Still, many people wonder if children really need such a heavy dose of violence and fear-provoking stories in a world that is frightening enough on its own. To use the words of child psychologist David Elkind, we live in the day of the "hurried child."[15] He argues that we try to rush our children into adulthood by exposing them to ideas and experiences for which they are not emotionally prepared. I know of parents who are proud of the fact that they buy toys, videos, or books for their children that state on their packaging that they are intended for older children. They let their eight- or nine-year-olds watch movies with a PG-13 rating. Although they know the concerns that others present, they like to think that their youngsters are the rare exception to the rule. Other parents simply give in to their children's pleas and let them watch or read whatever they want. J. K. Rowling herself has been surprised that parents have let their six- and seven-year-olds read her books, and she has actively discouraged parents from buying *Harry Potter and the Goblet of Fire* for their younger children, as some passages deal with sadistic torture and murder. Just because children are academically able to read and comprehend the words, it does not mean that they are emotionally prepared for the content of all books.

Films bring frightening and violent scenes to life in a graphic way. Although the imagination of a young reader can at times make a frightening scene easier to handle, a graphic scene in a film can evoke nightmares. The impact of these scenes is multiplied by repeated viewings of movies on videotape and DVD. Today's young viewers watch their favorite films again and again. Is it helpful for these frightening scenes to be a recurring part of their vision of the world? The film version of *The Lord of the Rings: The Fellowship of the Ring,* for example, is rated PG-13. This film features mature themes, some graphic violence, and intense loss. The film version of *Harry Potter and the Chamber of Secrets* is much darker and more frightening than the first Harry Potter film. There is simply no reason younger children need to watch these films.

I have a colleague who has a creative solution to some of these concerns. With the way many stories are marketed to young children, his son gets very excited about seeing certain films that have scenes his father considers to be too violent or too intense. If my friend feels the film still has some positive value, he purchases a copy of the video, hooks up a videotape player to a video recorder, edits out some of the more frightening or otherwise inappropriate scenes, and then lets his son watch it. (It is important to emphasize that my friend does this with his own copy of the movie and for his own private home use. It would be illegal and unethical to copy a rented film or to distribute his re-edited version in any way.) I have done this in a more basic way by showing only selected scenes to my children, while skipping or fast forwarding past others. The children get to see some of the fun scenes of dinosaurs or other creatures, and get a sense of what all the excitement is about. They also learn the lesson that while some films or videos are not necessarily bad, some things are inappropriate for them at a young age.

Should we let our children read and watch these stories as a way to process their frightening world? Or should we protect them from material that may not be suitable for them? Again, each person must discern her or his own answer. In any case, parents and concerned adults should take the time to preview what their children read and watch so they can make informed decisions. By previewing material, adults are prepared to discuss it with their children and to help them process the frightening parts as well as the themes of the stories. Hopefully, this book will help parents and teachers in this effort. We need to assure our children that they are safe and that they do not live in a world with dementors or Dark Riders around every corner. We need to let them know that they can always talk to us about their fears and about what they watch and read and experience in life.

Violent Resolutions

As we have seen in previous chapters, the Harry Potter stories, the *Star Wars* films, and *The Lord of the Rings* all promote the idea that evil is overcome by love and sacrifice, and not by the violent use of power. Still—perhaps ironically—these stories present heroes who carry swords and use them to lash out at their enemies, carrying the implicit message that violence *is* the answer. This is not surprising. Mythic stories, after all, are in part humankind's attempt to make concrete our abstract, internal struggles. Film in particular is a medium that tends to present conflicts as dramatic visual battles. The novel version of *The Two Towers,* for example, is quite thoughtful and deeply spiritual, featuring a number of extended conversations. The film version, on the other hand, plays largely as an epic war film that focuses on the battle scenes.

What message do these violent battles send to viewers? Because the violence is placed in a fantasy context, we may not be as concerned about copycat violence as we might be with the latest action-adventure thriller. It is unlikely that our children will pick up real swords or lightsabers and start slashing people. Still, today's fantasy stories contain a number of scenes that glamorize violence. Our heroes stab swords through the heads of basilisks, cut the arms off of aliens, and slash the heads off of orcs. And they look powerful and noble when doing so. Though the explicit themes of these stories may suggest that might does not make right, the implicit message may be that being quick to take violent action is a noble thing to do.

A more profound concern with violent content has to do with the message these stories send about how we resolve conflicts with other people in our lives. Fantasy stories have clear-cut heroes and evil opponents. The way conflict is resolved in these stories is simply by defeating the opponent. This is not the case only in today's fantasy stories. Popular Disney films also present the world in these terms. In *Beauty and the Beast* (1991), *The Lion King* (1994), and *The Hunchback of Notre Dame* (1996), to name just a few examples, the enemy is not only defeated but killed before the conflict is resolved. In these stories the world is divided between those who are good (us!) and those who are bad, and it seems like the only way to resolve any conflict is to destroy the enemy.

In the film *The Lord of the Rings: The Two Towers,* Sam Gamgee says, "There is some good in this world, Mr. Frodo, and it's worth fighting for." This is true. But as Sam and Frodo themselves demonstrate, there are nonviolent ways to fight for what is good. We know that in the real world, conflict is usually not resolved through violence. And as Christians we certainly do not want our children to be quick to view others as enemies or to believe that violence is the primary way to resolve conflict. In the fantasy genre, enemies are often quite literally demonized. But we need to discuss with our children that most of our conflicts will be with friends, family members, coworkers, and members of our church congregations. They are not demons, and it is not helpful to turn them into enemies or to try to defeat them. They are our friends. Even when we are dealing with people who are different from us, we are called to strive for peace and understanding rather than conflict and strife (Heb. 12:14). As Christians we strive to resolve our conflicts not by defeating our enemies but through honesty, understanding, grace, and forgiveness. Ours is the way of redemptive sacrifice, not the way of redemptive violence.

Concerns of Offending Others

Some Christians avoid these stories not because of any concerns of their own but because they want to avoid offending others. They take this as a normative principle, based on Paul's instructions regarding food sacrificed to idols, in his first letter to the Corinthians. He suggests that the Corinthian Christians should refrain from eating food sacrificed to idols for the sake of weak believers (1 Cor. 8:7–13). This passage has been misunderstood over the years, and has been interpreted to mean that any member of a congregation who is more restrictive in their approach to the Christian life than other members may be has veto power over the life practices of others. But Paul was passionately opposed to limiting the freedom we have in Christ just to appease another's opinion (Gal. 2:11–14, 5:2–12). He was simply concerned with confusing new Christians about adherence to pagan practices. If mature Christians continued to eat the meat of sacrificed idols—even if it was only for practical reasons—new Christians might believe that idol worship was compatible with Christianity.

To draw the analogy back to the practice of reading Harry Potter books today, it would be hard to imagine that a new Christian would think that we were actively practicing witchcraft or endorsing it as a religion consistent with Christianity just because we were reading Harry Potter books. As a matter of fact, most of those who are upset that others are reading the Harry Potter books are clear in their own mind as to the difference between the occult and Christianity. They are not about to stumble into the occult because of other people's reading habits.

How, then, would the principle found in Paul's instructions to the Corinthians apply to a situation in which someone complains about people reading the Harry Potter books? Should we desist so that we do not offend them? Two examples might help: When I served as a pastor, some teenage girls who were not members of our church came along on a youth-group camping trip. They were also relatively new to the whole concept of the Christian faith. Their mother actively practiced Wicca, and it became clear that the girls were not aware of any contradictions between Wicca and Christianity. They thought they could embrace the Christian faith and still embrace Wicca. Although my experience with these girls predated Harry Potter, I doubt that they would have thought that by reading Harry Potter books, other members of the youth group were practicing Wiccans. If I was concerned at all, I could simply talk to them and explain my beliefs. Still, for the sake of the girls, I would be sure that members of the group avoided actions that might be misunderstood as an endorsement of witchcraft or Wicca.

The second example does not involve someone who was new to the faith, but someone who was clear in his own mind what his Christian faith entailed. When I was in seminary, I put up a poster of the members of the Fellowship of the Ring. Most of my fellow students commented on how much they liked it, and we would talk about Tolkien's books and essays. One student, however, happened to come by and see it, and said that he was offended. He explained that some people who read *The Lord of the Rings* started to play Dungeons and Dragons, and that some people who played Dungeons and Dragons embraced the occult. According to his logic, then, *The Lord of the Rings* promoted the occult, and he felt that I should take the poster down. He said he was not concerned that people at the seminary would be led astray, but he was personally offended that I would read *The Lord of the Rings*. The situation troubled me, and I asked my seminary friends what I should do. I was ready to take the poster down, but my friends encouraged me to keep it up. They said that the student who complained was not in danger of being confused about the nature of the Christian faith. He knew that Christianity and witchcraft were inconsistent, and he knew that reading *The Lord of the Rings* did not mean that I was part of the occult. My friends were concerned, like Paul, that others should not be able to limit our freedom in Christ simply because they may choose to live out more restrictive expressions of their faith.

Still, Paul warns Christians, "Knowledge puffs up, but love builds up" (1 Cor. 8:1). We should not act superior to or contemptuous of those who are distressed by our actions. In my example, I made sure not to throw the poster in his face, mock his concerns, or put him down when talking to others.

Do you know of anyone in your congregation or community who may actually get the impression that Christians endorse witchcraft because you read these books or watch the films? Most likely your answer is no. But even so, we need to be careful to respect each other's concerns and not become arrogant in the freedom we have in Christ.

Obsession with the Fantasy Lands

Some people are so drawn into the complex fantasy worlds created by today's fantasy books and films that they do not want to leave. They talk of nothing else and seem to want to think of nothing else. What is the difference between a healthy interest and an unhealthy obsession?

Most child psychologists say that it is healthy for children to have hobbies and interests. By focusing on one type of television show or one line of toys, children gain mastery over a fictional world and gain confidence as they interact with the real world. But most psychologists would also warn against the dangers of a hobby that has turned into an obsession. If a child gets so far into these fantasy stories that she or he finds it hard to make it back to the real world, it is time to wean her or him from these books and films and perhaps seek out professional counseling.

Even when we are not in danger of becoming obsessed with these stories, at times we would do well to add some balance to our lives. There are some good *Star Wars* novels, for example, but hopefully that is not the only kind of literature we read. Some Tolkien fans have read *The Lord of the Rings* a dozen times or more, but fail to find the time to read the Bible or classic literature such as Victor Hugo's *Les Miserables* or Charles Dickens's *A Tale of Two Cities*. Some people watch the *Star Wars* films again and again, but do not take the opportunity to watch great films such as *On the Waterfront*,

Lilies of the Field, Sounder, Chariots of Fire, or *Babette's Feast.* If today's fantasy stories have enriched our lives, we can also benefit from branching out into classic works of fiction and film. We need to guard against allowing our passion for these stories to consume all our spare time and money. God has given us much more than these fantasy stories to experience and enjoy in this wondrous world.

In *Harry Potter and the Sorcerer's Stone,* Harry is fascinated by the Mirror of Erised, which shows him the deepest desire of his heart. He feels that he could stay there for days, imagining himself as part of the world inside the mirror. But Professor Dumbledore warns him of the dangers of doing so. He says to Harry, "It does not do to dwell on dreams and forget to live, remember that."[16]

There are many lessons to be learned and much to be enjoyed in the Harry Potter stories, the *Star Wars* films, *The Hobbit,* and *The Lord of the Rings* trilogy. These stories can help us reflect on our faith journey and embolden us for the tasks before us. But we cannot forget that these are fictional worlds. We cannot forget that we are called to come home from these worlds and enter fully into our own. We each have our own calling to live out in the real world. Our own journey with God is the most amazing adventure of all.

Questions for Reflection

Which of the concerns discussed in this chapter worry you the most? Which of the concerns worry you the least?

What concerns do you have about these stories that are not discussed in this chapter?

Which other popular books or films—even Christian books and films—concern you?

Do you know of anyone who is at risk of practicing witchcraft or joining an occult group? What can you do to express your concern? Where can you find more information about these groups?

How old do you think children should be before they watch or read these stories? How would you handle the situation if your six-year-old child or grandchild asked you if he or she could watch one of these films?

Recall a conflict you have had with someone at work, at home, or at your church. How was that conflict resolved? Did it help matters or hurt matters to look on the other person as an enemy?

Do you know of anyone who is offended by your interest in fantasy books or films? If so, what is their concern? How have you addressed it?

Do you know of anyone who is in danger of getting lost in these fantasy lands? How might you help him or her find the way home?

Notes

Introduction: Christian Approaches to Fantasy and Fiction

1. For a full treatment of this argument, see Russell W. Dalton, "Electronic Areopagus: Communicating the Gospel in Electronic Culture," *Journal of Theology,* Summer 1999, 17–34.

2. Elizabeth D. Schafer, *Exploring Harry Potter* (Osprey, FL: Beacham Publishing, 2000), 33.

3. Schafer, 26.

4. "Of Myth and Men: A conversation between Bill Moyers and George Lucas on the meaning of the Force and the true theology of *Star Wars,*" *Time,* April 26, 1999, 92.

5. "The Mythology of *Star Wars* with George Lucas and Bill Moyers," (Princeton, NJ: FFH Home Video, 2000, 57 minutes).

6. J. R. R. Tolkien, Letter to W. H. Auden on May 12, 1965, as quoted in Colin Duriez, *The J. R. R. Tolkien Handbook: A Concise Guide to His Life, Writings, and World of Middle-Earth* (Grand Rapids, Mich.: Baker Books, 1992), 62.

7. See Michael Medved, *Hollywood vs. America* (New York: HarperCollins Publishers/Zondervan, 1992).

8. J. K. Rowling, *Harry Potter and the Chamber of Secrets* (New York: Scholastic Press, 1998), 72.

9. Rowling, *Harry Potter and the Goblet of Fire* (New York: Scholastic Press, 2000), 395.

10. This is not the case with every contemporary fantasy novel. Phillip Pullman's *His Dark Materials* trilogy, for example, can be seen as a passionate and somewhat troubling negative critique of the Christian faith, or at least organized Christian religion. The trilogy includes Phillip Pullman, *The Golden Compass* (New York: Alfred A. Knopf, 1995); Pullman, *The Subtle Knife* (New York: Alfred A. Knopf, 1997); Pullman, *The Amber Spyglass* (New York: Alfred A. Knopf, 2000).

11. See, for example, Ted Bahr's *The Media-Wise Family* (Colorado Springs, Colo.: Chariot-Victor Publishing, 1998) and his monthly *Movie Guide.*

12. "Why we like Harry Potter: The series is a 'Book of Virtues' with a preadolescent funny bone." *Christianity Today,* January 10, 2000. See also their film review by Douglas LeBlanc, "Somewhat wild about Harry: It's well nigh impossible to hate the warm-hearted Harry Potter," *Christianity Today,* January 7, 2002, vol. 46, no. 1, 68.

13. See, for example, Richard Abanes, *Harry Potter and the Bible: The Menace behind the Magik* (Camp Hill, Penn.: Horizon Books, 2001).

14. The "thumbs up" or "thumbs down" approach was famously used by Roger Ebert and Gene Siskel on their show *Siskel and Ebert at the Movies.* Ironically, although Siskel and Ebert became known for the thumbs up or down reviews, both were accomplished film critics who in their columns contributed excellent, nuanced reviews.

15. Bryan P. Stone, *Faith and Film: Theological Themes at the Cinema* (St. Louis, Mo.: Chalice Press, 2000), 7.

16. For more on this approach, see Pamela Mitchell Legg, "Contemporary Film and Religious Exploration: An Opportunity for Religious Education. Part I: Foundational Questions," *Religious Education,* 91 no. 3 (Summer 1996), 397–406; and Mitchell Legg, "Contemporary Film and Religious Exploration: An Opportunity for Religious Education. Part II: How to Engage in Conversation with Film," *Religious Education,* 92 no. 1 (Winter 1997), 120–131.

17. Such as, for example, Joseph Campbell, *The Hero with a Thousand Faces.*

18. "The Mythology of *Star Wars* with George Lucas and Bill Moyers," (Princeton, N.J.: FFH Home Video, 2000, 57 minutes).

19. Tolkien, "On Fairy Stories," in *The Tolkien Reader* (New York: Ballantine Books, 1966), 72.

20. C. S. Lewis, *They Stand Together: The Letters of C. S. Lewis to Arthur Greeves, 1914–1963,* edited by Walter Hooper (New York: MacMillan, 1979), 427.

21. Ibid.

22. Please note that I use the word *hero* to refer to both male and female protagonists.

23. The Bible is a big book, and we are in danger any time we quote a verse or two and then suggest that we have "proof-texted" it or presented *the* biblical view of one topic or the other. My desire is to make a few connections between these stories of today and some passages of the Bible. But to understand the "biblical" view on any issue, our best option is to read the books of the Bible themselves from beginning to end.

Chapter 1: A Whole New World

1. Rowling, *Quidditch through the Ages* (New York: Arthur A. Levine Books, 2001).

2. Rowling, *Fantastic Beasts and Where to Find Them* (New York: Arthur A. Levine Books, 2001).

3. George R. R. Martin, "Introduction," in *Meditations on Middle Earth,* Karen Haber, ed. (New York: St. Martin's Press, 2001), 3.

4. Rowling, *Harry Potter and the Sorcerer's Stone* (New York: Scholastic Press, 1997).

5. This is the title of the very first *Star Wars* film that was released in 1977, which is most commonly known simply as *Star Wars.* The title *Star Wars: A New Hope* has been used since that initial release to distinguish it from the other *Star Wars* films. Although this film was the first one released in the series, it is also referred to as "Episode IV," as the events in the film occur after the events of episodes 1 through 3.

6. J. R. Baxter Jr., "This World Is Not My Home," in *Sentimental Songs,* (Stamps-Baxter Music and Printing Co.), 1946.

7. Rowling, *Harry Potter and the Sorcerer's Stone,* 291.

8. Tolkien, *The Fellowship of the Ring,* 2nd ed. (Boston: Houghton Mifflin Company, 1965).

9. Tolkien, *The Fellowship of the Ring,* 281.

10. For a more in-depth exploration of this concern, see the "Dangers Along the Path" section of this book.

11. William Shakespeare, *Hamlet,* Act i, Scene 5.

12. Cf. Lewis, *Miracles* (San Francisco: Harper and Row, 1947).

13. Tolkien, *The Fellowship of the Ring,* 377.

14. Ibid., 378.

15. Rowling, *Harry Potter and the Sorcerer's Stone,* 302.

16. Cf. Tolkien, *The Fellowship of the Ring,* 65.

Chapter 2: A Call to Journey

1. Tolkien, *The Hobbit,* 4th ed. (Boston: Houghton Mifflin Company, 1966).

2. Ibid., 13.

3. Ibid., 14.

4. Rowling, *Harry Potter and the Sorcerer's Stone,* 287.

5. It is worth noting that not everyone wants to be special. In *Harry Potter and the Sorcerer's Stone,* we learn that the Dursleys wanted desperately to be perfectly normal. In contrast, Jesus came to give us an abundant life (John 10:10).

6. Tolkien, *The Two Towers,* 2nd ed. (Boston: Houghton Mifflin Company, 1954, 1965), 321.

7. Tolkien, *The Fellowship of the Ring* (Boston: Houghton Mifflin Company, 1954, 1965), 284.

8. Ibid., 70.

9. Ibid. In the film *The Lord of the Rings: The Fellowship of the Rings,* Lady Galadriel speaks these words to Frodo.

10. Cf. Tolkien, *The Fellowship of the Ring,* 60.

Chapter 3: Learning the Way

1. Rowling, *Harry Potter and the Order of the Phoenix* (New York: Scholastic Press, 2003), 240.

2. Ibid., 243.

3. Rowling, *Harry Potter and the Sorcerer's Stone*, 287.

Chapter 4: Travel Provisions

1. Rowling, *Harry Potter and the Sorcerer's Stone*, 299.

Chapter 5: Traveling Companions

1. Rowling, *Harry Potter and the Sorcerer's Stone*, 287.

2. Rowling, *Harry Potter and the Prisoner of Azkaban* (New York: Scholastic Books, 1999), 274.

3. "The Mythology of *Star Wars* with George Lucas and Bill Moyers."

4. Cf. Sam K. Williams, "friendship," *HarperCollins Bible Dictionary*, Paul J. Achetemeier, ed. (San Francisco: HarperCollins, 1996), 352.

5. Tolkien, *Return of the King*, 2nd ed. (Boston: Houghton Mifflin Company, 1955, 1965).

6. Rowling, *Harry Potter and the Sorcerer's Stone*, 109.

7. Tolkien, *The Return of the King*, 116.

8. Tolkien, *The Fellowship of the Ring*, 182.

Chapter 6: Staying on the Right Path

1. Tolkien, *The Two Towers*, 322.

2. Rowling, *Harry Potter and the Sorcerer's Stone*, 121.

3. Rowling, *Harry Potter and the Chamber of Secrets*, 333.

4. Rowling, *Harry Potter and the Sorcerer's Stone*, 294.

Chapter 7: Road Signs

1. "The Mythology of *Star Wars* with George Lucas and Bill Moyers."

2. Cf. Tolkien, *Fellowship of the Ring*, 68–69.

Chapter 8: Creatures of the Dark

1. Rowling, *Harry Potter and the Prisoner of Azkaban*, 221.

Chapter 9: Rough Roads Ahead

1. Karl Marx, *A Contribution to the Critique of Hegel's Philosophy of Right* (1844), preface.

2. Rowling, *Harry Potter and the Order of the Phoenix*, 863.

3. Ibid., 861.

4. Rowling, *Harry Potter and the Sorcerer's Stone*, 297.

5. Rowling, *Harry Potter and the Goblet of Fire*, 724.

Chapter 10: The Trail of Trials

1. See Joseph Campbell, *The Hero with a Thousand Faces*, 2nd ed. (Princeton, N.J.: Princeton University Press, 1968), 97ff.

2. For example, Bruno Bettelheim, *The Uses of Enchantment* (New York, Alfred A. Knopf, 1976), 94, 217–220.

3. Campbell, 91.

Chapter 11: The Way of Christ

1. For a recent Christian fantasy that uses this image to tell the Christ story, see Calvin Miller, *The Singer* (Downers Grove, Ill.: InterVarsity Press, 1979).

2. Rowling, *Harry Potter and the Sorcerer's Stone*, 299.

3. This strong magic is what C. S. Lewis called "the Deep Magic" in *The Lion, the Witch, and the Wardrobe* (New York: MacMillan Publishing, 1950), 138–141.

4. At least Obi-Wan's sacrifice is clearly intended to function in a way that saves his friends. Actually, many viewers have found it difficult to see how Obi-Wan's sacrifice actually helped the situation until he returned in spirit form.

5. Tolkien, *The Return of the King*, 139.

Chapter 12: There and Back Again

1. Tolkien, *The Return of the King*, 311.

Special Section: Dangers along the Path

1. "Why we like Harry Potter: The series is a 'Book of Virtues' with a preadolescent funny bone," *Christianity Today*, January 10, 2000. See also their film review by Douglas LeBlanc, "Somewhat wild about Harry: It's well nigh impossible to hate the warm-hearted Harry Potter," *Christianity Today*, January 7, 2002, vol. 46, no. 1, 68.

2. Chuck Colson, "Witches and wizards: The Harry Potter phenomenon," *Breakpoint*, November 2, 1999.

3. God in a Galaxy Far, Far, Away: The *Star Wars* Christian Fan Fiction Project, found at http://www.geocities.com/Area51/Keep/1133/fanfic/

4. Associated Press, "Rings' film wins Tolkien more Christian fans," *The Hollywood Reporter*, January 25, 2002.

5. See Elizabeth D. Schafer, *Exploring Harry Potter*, 33, and for a variety of links to articles and information, see "Religion and the *Harry Potter* series FAQ" page of HpforGrownups, at http://groups.yahoo.com/group/HPforGrownups/. The specific address is http://www.i2k.com/~svderark/lexicon/faq/religion.html#fnlnk0013.

6. Schafer, 206.

7. Incidentally, the Narnia series has some strong connections to today's popular fantasy stories as well. J. R. R. Tolkien was a good friend of Lewis', as Lewis wrote the Chronicles of Narnia and Tolkien wrote *The Lord of the Rings*. Rowling has stated that she loved the series, and that they have influenced her writing and are one of the reasons she chose to make her series last for seven books.

8. For a good, balanced article discussing these concerns, see Kimbra Wilder Gish, "Hunting down Harry Potter: An exploration of religious concerns about children's literature," *The Horn Book Magazine*, 262–271.

9. It is worth noting that the same principle applies to New Age groups that use the *Star Wars* films to promote their religious outlooks. As explained in the introduction of this book, George Lucas did not intend his films to serve as examples of any one religion, but many New Age religions have done more to draw connections to their beliefs than most Christian churches have.

10. "Why we like Harry Potter: The series is a 'Book of Virtues' with a preadolescent funny bone," *Christianity Today*, January 10, 2000, and Michael G. Maudlin, "Virtue on a broomstick," (September 4, 2000), 117–119.

11. Rowling, *Harry Potter and the Chamber of Secrets*, 289.

12. Rowling, *Harry Potter and the Goblet of Fire*, 207.

13. Rowling, *Harry Potter and the Chamber of Secrets*, 333.

14. Bruno Bettelheim, *The Uses of Enchantment: The Meaning and Importance of Fairy Tales* (New York: Alfred A. Knopf, 1976).

15. See David Elkind's *The Hurried Child*, 3rd ed. (Cambridge, Mass.: Perseus Books, 2001).

16. Rowling, *Harry Potter and the Sorcerer's Stone*, 214.

Fantasy Land Index

Harry Potter

Star Wars

The Lord of the Rings

Fantasy Books and Films

Scripture Index

Hebrew Scriptures

Christian Scriptures

Other Resources from Augsburg

Video, Kids, and Christian Education by Russell W. Dalton
72 pages, 0-8066-6410-X

Our children are immersed in a TV culture. This book lists many suggestions for appropriately incorporating video to help add sights and sounds to the gospel message.

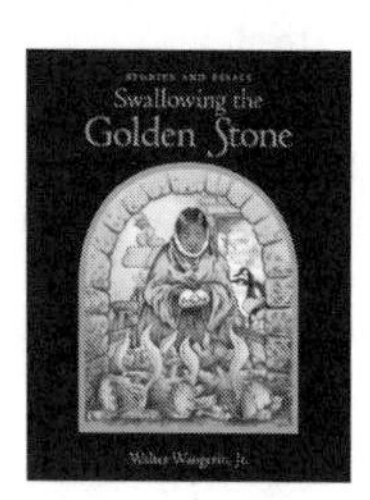

Swallowing the Golden Stone by Walter Wangerin, Jr.
184 pages, 0-8066-3710-2

An illustrated collection of Wangerin's rich and original fairy tales, including *Branta and the Golden Stone* and *Elisabeth and the Water Troll,* plus fresh and insightful essays on writing, reading, story, and faith.

A Joyful Theology by Sara Maitland
144 pages, 0-8066-4473-7

A lively exploration of creation to learn more about the Creator. The author finds a God who inspires awe, who calls us to be committed to one another, and who invites us to live in joy.

God Is Love edited by Brian Doyle
152 pages, 0-8066-4449-4

God Is Love brings together diverse voices of recognized writers on the common ground of spirituality. In this book, more than two dozen writers share a variety of reflections on spiritual life.

Available wherever books are sold.